ChatGPT for Business 101

AI-Driven Strategies to Cut Costs, Skyrocket Productivity and Boost Your Bottom Line

Russel Grant

Contents

Introduction

As the sun began to set behind the horizon, casting a warm glow over the tranquil scenery, I couldn't help but marvel at how far my business had come. It felt like just yesterday when I was struggling to keep up with the demands of running a growing furniture business. Back then, the idea of using AI to streamline my operations seemed like a distant dream. The rise of social media and online advertising sounds foreign, one that I struggled to understand as an old-fashioned craftsman.

When I first encountered ChatGPT, I was hesitant, skeptical of its capabilities, and unsure of how it could fit into my traditional, hands-on approach to business. Yet, with each prompt and response, I witnessed the power of AI unfold before my eyes. It was as if a window had been opened to a world of endless possibilities where creativity knew no bounds. My first book on Prompt Engineering and ChatGPT chronicled my initial skepticism and eventual adoption of AI technology, which changed how I approached marketing and content creation for my business today.

Since then, I have used ChatGPT to craft engaging social media posts, write compelling email campaigns, and even create product descriptions. Its ability to generate content and ideas that resonated with my audience helped me expand my reach far beyond my local town, attracting customers from across the country.

ChatGPT has changed everything. The time saved through automation has helped me focus more on designing and crafting new pieces, pushing the boundaries of my creativity further than ever before. Looking back, I realized that embracing AI was the best decision I have ever made for my business.

Steering a business in today's digital world feels like running a never-ending marathon, doesn't it? With fierce competition at every turn and customers expecting the moon, it seems like you're constantly being pulled in a million directions. Cutting operational costs while boosting productivity and innovation isn't just a goal—it's your daily challenge. But what if there's a powerful ally that can not only help you meet these challenges but turn them into your biggest opportunities for growth?

Imagine being able to handle customer inquiries, personalize marketing campaigns, and boost operational efficiency—all with the help of AI. This is the promise of ChatGPT for business. Small businesses and industry giants like Slack, Shopify, Coca-Cola, Snap Inc., etc., are exploring the power of AI to enhance customer satisfaction and stay ahead in this digital age.

According to Strata, 46% of American companies have saved between \$25,000 and \$70,000 by using ChatGPT (Statista, 2023). Take Nutella, for example; they launched an advertising campaign where they used AI to create 7 million unique Nutella jar labels—each jar with a one-of-a-kind design. This AI-driven campaign tapped into customers' desire for uniqueness and personalization with every single jar of Nutella sold.

Despite the undeniable benefits, you may still perceive AI as a distant, complex frontier reserved only for the tech elite. If you've ever found yourself thinking, "AI sounds like a hassle," or "Tech isn't my forte; how am I supposed to use this?" or if you have ever thought that AI is too complex or that it wasn't for you, think again. AI and ChatGPT are more within your grasp than ever before, ready to blend into your business operations, no matter your business size or tech-savvy.

But here's the kicker: while you have undoubtedly heard of ChatGPT and its 180 million user base and 1.7 billion monthly site views as of December 2023, you may still be struggling with how to leverage this technology to its fullest potential in your business. That's where *ChatGPT for Business 101* comes in.

This book is an essential guide to everything about ChatGPT in the business world, as it provides practical guidance and strategies to help scale your growing business. You will learn how to integrate cost-effective chatbots into your business operation to provide personalized assistance, answer customer queries, and streamline support processes for a seamless customer experience. You will also discover techniques for boosting conversion rates in e-commerce through targeted messaging and recommendations while using AI to analyze customer behavior and tailor marketing strategies to drive sales and increase revenue.

With *ChatGPT for Business 101*, you will gain a deep understanding of AI and ChatGPT applications, learn tips for implementation, and gain insights into optimizing content creation, from crafting engaging social media posts to generating converting email campaigns that captivate your audience and enhance brand visibility. Whether you are a seasoned entrepreneur or just starting out, this book will help you stay ahead of the curve and grow in the business world.

And what result should you expect? A business that runs smoother, engages customers more effectively, and outshines the competition while you feel confident and equipped to tackle any obstacle that comes your way in your business. So, if you are tired of struggling with inefficiency and lackluster results and ready to take your business to the next level, then let's embark on this exciting learning journey together.

1. The Dawn of Artificial Intelligence in Business

In the not-so-distant past, the notion of artificial intelligence (AI) seemed like something out of a science fiction novel—an interesting concept that belonged to the realm of imagination, not reality. Yet, today, AI has become an integral part of our everyday lives, changing the way we work, communicate, and interact with the world around us.

Nowhere is this transformation more evident than in the world of business. Over the past decade, AI has rapidly evolved from a novelty to a necessity, reshaping industries, redefining business models, and restructuring the way companies operate.

According to IBM, businesses that have adopted AI technologies are experiencing up to a 40% improvement in efficiency and a notable increase in customer satisfaction rates. For instance, Netflix uses AI algorithms to analyze user behavior and offer personalized content recommendations. This strategy has led to a 30% increase in user retention and a significant 40%

increase in viewing hours. As a result, customers are more engaged, spend longer periods on the platform, and are more likely to recommend Netflix to others. These are not just incremental improvements; they are capable of elevating a business in today's hyper-competitive marketplace.

AI tools like ChatGPT are helping businesses communicate with their customers and streamline their operations. As we move on in this chapter, we will explore the impact of AI and ChatGPT on the business world and why understanding and integrating these technologies is no longer optional but essential for business success and competitiveness. We will look into real-world examples of how businesses are leveraging AI to gain a competitive edge, drive growth, and enhance customer experiences. We will also discuss the practical steps that businesses can take to adopt AI and ChatGPT to unlock new opportunities and achieve sustainable growth in the digital age, just like I did.

The Role of AI in Business

Artificial intelligence (AI) refers to the ability of a computer or computer-controlled robot to perform tasks that typically require human intelligence. This includes tasks such as reasoning, problem-solving, understanding language, and learning from experience. AI aims to replicate human-like cognitive functions in machines, which can involve developing algorithms and systems that can process information, draw conclusions, and make decisions based on that information. One key aspect of AI is its ability to learn from past experiences. This is known as machine learning, a subset of AI that focuses on developing algorithms that improve automatically through experience.

Artificial intelligence, once the "stuff" of science fiction, has become a reality in the business world. From customer service chatbots to predictive analytics, AI is at the beck and call of today's businesses. According to a report by PwC, AI is expected to contribute up to $15.7 trillion to the global economy by 2030, making it one of the most significant drivers of economic growth in the coming decade.

One of the key reasons for the rapid adoption of AI in business is its ability to automate mundane and repetitive tasks, allowing your employees to focus on other activities. The use of AI in businesses is beyond what you can imagine or think of. However, let's look at how AI and ChatGPT are used in business today.

Content Generation

One of the key ways AI is used in content generation is through natural language processing (NLP) models like ChatGPT. These models are trained on vast amounts of text data and are capable of generating human-like text based on the prompt you input into it. This enables businesses to create blog posts, articles, product descriptions, and other types of content quickly and efficiently.

For example, a marketing team could use ChatGPT to generate social media posts or email newsletters, saving time and resources compared to writing them manually. Similarly, a content creator could use AI to generate ideas or outlines for articles, helping them overcome writer's block and stay productive. Another use case for AI in content generation is content optimization. AI-powered tools can analyze existing content and provide recommendations for improving readability, SEO, and engagement. Likewise, ChatGPT can suggest relevant keywords, meta tags, and content structures to improve SEO rankings. Tools like MarketMuse, Jasper AI, SurferSEO, Frase, Scalenut, etc., use AI to analyze top-performing content and suggest ways to optimize your content for better results.

Marketing

Using AI and ChatGPT in marketing is a move forward in how businesses engage with their audience, personalize their messaging, and optimize their campaigns. One way to leverage these technologies is through content creation. AI can generate high-quality, relevant marketing copy, helping marketers maintain a consistent presence across different channels.

AI-powered chatbots can enhance customer interactions by providing instant responses to queries with personalized recommendations and even facilitating transactions. This improves customer satisfaction and can lead to increased sales and loyalty. Moving on, it can analyze customer data quickly and accurately and identify patterns and trends that can inform marketing strategies. For example, a clothing retailer can use AI to analyze customer data and see trends in fashion preferences. Based on this analysis, the retailer can create personalized recommendations for each customer, increasing the likelihood of a purchase.

Sales

In sales, you can use AI algorithms to analyze customer data, generate tailored product descriptions and promotional messages, and use past interactions to provide personalized product recommendations. AI can also use leads based on customers' behavior and interactions with your website or emails to prioritize high-potential leads. It can assist you in engaging with leads through automated messaging, providing information and assistance in real time.

Also, AI is efficient in using algorithms to analyze historical sales data and market trends to forecast future sales. Generating reports and insights based on this data can help the sales team in your company make informed decisions. AI tools like Levity, Incendium, and many others can help analyze customer preferences and behavior to personalize email marketing campaigns while you use ChatGPT to generate email content, subject lines, and call-to-action messages that resonate with customers.

Customer Service

Businesses can streamline interactions, resolve issues more quickly, and provide a more tailored experience for their customers by integrating these technologies into customer service operations. One way AI and ChatGPT are being integrated into customer service is through chatbots. These AI-powered assistants can handle routine inquiries, such as FAQs, product information, and basic troubleshooting. Chatbots provide 24/7 support, ensuring that customers always have access to assistance when they need it.

Another use case for AI and ChatGPT in customer service is in sentiment analysis. Through customer interactions, including emails, chat transcripts, and social media posts, AI algorithms can detect customer sentiment and identify potential issues before they escalate. This allows businesses to proactively address customer concerns and improve overall satisfaction.

IT Operations

AI is a trailblazing tool that can help you manage your tasks. For example, AI-powered chatbots provide instant support to employees, troubleshooting technical issues and answering queries in real time. This reduces the burden on IT support teams and improves overall efficiency.

Also, AI can be used to automate routine tasks, such as system monitoring and maintenance. AI algorithms detect anomalies and predict potential issues before they occur, allowing IT teams to address them even before they happen. As a business owner, you don't need to always send reminder emails to your workers about an upcoming meeting, as it can assist in project management, providing updates and reminders to your team members. With AI, you have time for other things, either personal or business-related.

Human Resources

Human resources (HR) departments are increasingly turning to AI and ChatGPT to enhance their effectiveness. One key application of AI in HR is in recruitment and talent acquisition. With detailed prompts, ChatGPT and other AI-powered tools can scrutinize resumes, screen candidates, and even conduct initial interviews. This saves HR professionals time and helps them identify the best candidates more efficiently.

AI in HR offers benefits in employee engagement and retention. AI-powered systems can use employee feedback, performance data, and other relevant metrics to identify patterns that can help HR teams better understand and address employee needs and concerns. This leads to higher employee satisfaction and lower turnover rates.

Cybersecurity

One of the many ways AI is used in cybersecurity is through the development of AI-powered threat detection systems. These systems work on large amounts of data to check for anomalies that may indicate a potential cyberattack. Organizations can use this to detect and respond to threats in real time, minimizing the impact of attacks.

You can also use AI in the development of AI-powered authentication systems. These systems use machine learning algorithms to examine user behavior and verify identities, making it more difficult for hackers to gain unauthorized access to systems and data.

Legal Department

In legal departments, AI-powered contract analysis tools are useful in quickly reviewing and extracting key information from contracts, saving time and reducing the risk of human error. Similarly, ChatGPT can assist lawyers in drafting legal documents, conducting legal research, and even providing legal advice to clients. Also, AIs can analyze legal data, such as case outcomes or judges' rulings, to assist lawyers in making more informed decisions.

Accounting and Finance

In accounting and finance, AI-powered tools can automate repetitive tasks, such as data entry and reconciliation. ChatGPT can be used to generate financial reports and provide insights that aid in decision-making. For example, AI algorithms can analyze financial data and make predictions about the performance of a product or the stock market. ChatGPT can also generate natural language summaries of financial reports, making it easier for stakeholders to understand complex financial information, detect fraudulent activities, and improve compliance with regulatory requirements.

The Evolution of AI

The evolution of artificial intelligence (AI) spans several decades and has been marked by significant advancements and breakthroughs. In the early 1950s, a groundbreaking idea took root in the minds of visionary scientists and mathematicians—a concept that would forever change the course of human history. This concept was artificial intelligence (AI), the notion that machines could be injected with intelligence akin to that of humans to help them reason, learn, and make decisions autonomously. Let's look through the beginning and growth of AI.

The Birth of AI (1950–1956)

The birth of AI can be traced back to 1950 when Alan Turing proposed the famous Turing Test, which aimed to determine a machine's ability to exhibit intelligent behavior indistinguishable from that of a human. This period also saw the creation of the first neural network-based learning machine by Marvin Minsky and Dean Edmonds, laying the groundwork for future AI research.

AI Maturation (1957–1979)

The late 1950s and 1960s witnessed significant advancements in AI, with the development of programs capable of solving algebra word problems and playing chess at a rudimentary level. In 1966, the first AI laboratory was established at Stanford University, which serves as the formalization of AI as a distinct field of study.

AI Boom (1980–1987)

The 1980s saw a surge of interest and investment in AI. This sudden surge was fueled by advancements in computer technology and the emergence of expert systems capable of mimicking human expertise in specific domains. During this period, there was the development of expert systems for medical diagnosis, financial forecasting, and other applications, showcasing AI's potential in different industries.

AI Winter (1987–1993)

The AI boom of the 1980s was short-lived, as unrealistic expectations and overhyped promises led to a period of anticlimax known as the AI winter. Funding for AI research dried up, and interest in the field waned as progress failed to meet expectations.

AI Agents (1993–2011)

The early 1990s marked a resurgence of interest in AI as there were increased advancements in machine learning and the development of intelligent agents capable of autonomous decision-making. This period saw the emergence of AI applications in areas such as data mining, natural language processing, and robotics, paving the way for AI's integration into mainstream business operations.

AI General Intelligence

In recent years, the concept of artificial general intelligence (AGI), or AI with human-level intelligence across a wide range of domains, has gained prominence. While AGI remains a distant goal, advancements in deep learning, neural networks, and other AI technologies have brought us closer to achieving this ambitious vision.

The evolution of AI from its rudimentary stage to its current state has significantly influenced business operations. In 2022, OpenAI released ChatGPT, a groundbreaking AI-powered conversational agent that is now the fastest-growing consumer internet app of all time. ChatGPT's ability to engage in natural, human-like conversations has transformed customer service, marketing, sales, and other business functions, helping organizations deliver personalized experiences at scale and revolutionizing the way they interact with customers and stakeholders. As businesses continue to embrace AI technologies like ChatGPT, the future promises even greater opportunities for innovation and growth in the business world.

ChatGPT Chatbot vs. ChatGPT API

ChatGPT offers two distinct ways to interact with its powerful language processing capabilities. Understanding the difference between the ChatGPT chatbot and the ChatGPT API is important for choosing the right approach for your needs.

The Conversationalist: ChatGPT Chatbot

ChatGPT chatbot is like a friendly, ever-learning companion you can chat with. It is a readily available interface that is accessible directly through OpenAI's website. This user-friendly platform allows anyone to engage in conversation with the AI and ask questions across diverse topics.

The beauty of the ChatGPT chatbot lies in its simplicity. It doesn't require any technical expertise—you simply start typing, and the conversation unfolds. This makes it ideal for casual exploration. If you're curious about what ChatGPT can do, the chatbot is a fantastic starting point. You can experiment with different prompts and questions, getting a feel for its fluency and range of responses. Or idea generation as a brainstorming partner, generating new ideas for stories, poems, or marketing slogans. Or simple question-and-answer for basic questions that don't require in-depth analysis.

The Powerhouse: ChatGPT API

While the chatbot offers a straightforward interaction, the real magic lies beneath the surface—the ChatGPT API. This API functions as the engine powering the chatbot, granting developers access to the core functionalities of ChatGPT.

Think of it like this: The chatbot is a prebuilt website you can visit and interact with, but you can't modify its design or features. The API, on the other hand, provides the building blocks (the code and functionalities) that developers can leverage to create entirely new applications.

With ChatGPT API, you can build chatbots tailored to specific purposes, like a customer service bot trained to answer product inquiries or a virtual assistant optimized for scheduling tasks. Developers have greater control over how ChatGPT is used. They can define specific parameters for the AI's responses, ensuring they align perfectly with the application's goals.

The API allows ChatGPT to be seamlessly integrated into existing applications. This could be used to enhance customer support systems, personalize marketing campaigns, or even develop educational tools powered by AI-driven explanations.

Real-Life Stories

Beyond this, let's look at some real-life examples of how multinational companies have integrated AI into their operations and taken advantage of what it offers to be ahead in this competitive digital age.

Alibaba

Alibaba Group is a multinational conglomerate specializing in e-commerce, retail, the internet, and technology. They faced the challenge of managing a large inventory and optimizing product recommendations to enhance user experience and drive sales.

However, with AI algorithms, including natural language processing (NLP) and machine learning, they were able to analyze customer behavior, preferences, and browsing history. This data was used to personalize product recommendations and tailor marketing strategies to individual users. Alibaba uses AI in its City Brain Project, Cloud Computing Division, and inventory management systems to optimize supply chain logistics, reduce costs, and improve overall operational efficiency.

Amazon

Amazon, a global leader in e-commerce and cloud computing, uses AI in many parts of its business. One of Amazon's stores, called Amazon Go, uses AI to track the items customers pick up. Customers don't need to check out; they just grab what they want and leave. Cameras in the store watch what customers take, and they are automatically charged for those items through the Amazon Go app on their phones. This makes shopping quicker and easier for customers.

Also, Amazon uses AI-driven inventory management tools to predict demand, leading to a 25% reduction in inventory carrying costs and a significant decrease in stockouts. This has resulted in higher customer satisfaction levels. The improved efficiency has also led to a 20% increase in fulfillment rates, allowing Amazon to deliver orders faster than ever.

Tencent

Tencent, a leading Chinese social media company, uses artificial intelligence (AI) in various aspects of its operations. With over 1 billion users on its app WeChat, Tencent has expanded into gaming, digital assistants, mobile payments, cloud storage, live streaming, sports, education, movies, and self-driving cars. The company reflects its commitment to integrating AI into its services by collecting data from its users to improve its products and services.

Tencent also uses AI-powered fraud detection and prevention systems that use user behavior, transaction patterns, and network activity to look out for suspicious activities in real time. These systems utilize machine learning algorithms to adapt and evolve based on emerging threats and evolving attack techniques.

This helps Tencent mitigate fraud risks and protect user data from unauthorized access and malicious activities while also reducing financial losses associated with fraudulent transactions and improving user trust and confidence in Tencent's platforms and services.

Addressing Common Misconceptions and Fears

Artificial intelligence (AI) has become a force today, yet there are still common misconceptions and fears surrounding its adoption. Let's debunk some of these myths:

Myth 1: GenAI Won't Affect My Business

Many businesses mistakenly believe that AI, particularly generative AI (GenAI), won't affect their operations. However, the reality is that AI is already reshaping industries across the board. Major software providers like Microsoft, Google, and Salesforce are integrating generative AI features into their software offerings. From customer service automation to data analysis and content generation, AI technologies like ChatGPT are becoming integral to business processes. This presents businesses with a unique opportunity to use AI technologies for increased efficiency, improved customer experiences, and enhanced decision-making processes.

Myth 2: It's So Massive, We Have to Go Slow

Some businesses fear that implementing AI requires massive overhauls and extensive investments, leading them to proceed cautiously or avoid adoption altogether. However, AI implementation doesn't have to be an all-or-nothing endeavor. Companies can start small, focusing on specific use cases or departments, and gradually scale their AI initiatives as they gain confidence and see positive results. Also, leveraging AIaaS (AI as a Service) solutions allows businesses to access AI capabilities without the need for significant upfront investments or infrastructure changes.

Myth 3: Generative AI Is Too New and Risky

While generative AI, which includes technologies like ChatGPT, is relatively new, it has already demonstrated its potential across various industries. Businesses may hesitate to embrace generative AI due to concerns about reliability, security, and ethical implications. However, advancements in AI research, coupled with rigorous testing and validation processes, have enhanced the reliability and safety of generative AI models. Moreover, by adhering to ethical guidelines and implementing robust security measures, you can mitigate potential risks and use generative AI to increase your business's overall performance.

Myth 4: Generative AI Will Replace Employees

Generative AI can indeed automate certain tasks and streamline processes, but it's unlikely to replace human employees entirely. Instead, AI serves as a complement to human work, augmenting capabilities to enhance productivity and efficiency. Using AI will help businesses automate repetitive tasks while employees can focus on higher-value work that requires human creativity and critical thinking.

Myth 5: We'll Need to Hire a Lot of New Talent for Generative AI

Although implementing AI may require some expertise in AI technologies, businesses don't necessarily need to hire a large number of new employees. Many AI tools and platforms are designed to be user-friendly and accessible. This allows existing employees to learn and use them without extensive technical knowledge. Also, businesses can take advantage of external resources, such as AI consultants or training programs, to support their AI initiatives without significant hiring costs.

Myth 6: We Don't Need Generative AI for Our Digital Transformation

In today's rapidly evolving business world, digital transformation is essential for staying competitive and meeting customer demands. AI plays a crucial role in digital transformation by allowing businesses to innovate, personalize customer experiences, and create new revenue streams. It can be used to automate tasks, optimize processes, and drive business growth and success. Businesses that embrace AI are better positioned to stay competitive and adapt to the evolving digital landscape.

Setting the Stage for AI Integration

Integrating AI into your business can be both exciting and daunting, but with the right approach, it becomes an achievable and rewarding endeavor. To ensure a successful integration, it's important to follow a systematic approach. Here are ten steps to help your business start their AI journey:

Step 1: Find Out What AI Is All About

Begin by gaining a basic understanding of AI and its potential applications in your industry. Do your research and educate yourself and your team on the fundamentals of AI technologies and how they can benefit your business.

Step 2: Determine the Business Problem You Can Solve with AI

Identify specific challenges or opportunities within your business that AI can address. To do this, you need to understand the types of services your business provides. A problem, such as long wait times for customer support inquiries, can guide AI initiatives toward implementing a chatbot system to provide immediate assistance and reduce response times.

Step 3: Determine the Internal Capability

Assess your organization's existing capabilities and resources related to AI, including technical expertise, data infrastructure, and budget. Identify any gaps that need to be addressed to successfully implement AI solutions.

Step 4: Assess the Potential Value for AI Implementation

Evaluate the potential benefits and ROI of integrating AI into your business. Consider factors such as cost savings, efficiency gains, revenue growth, and competitive advantage to determine the value proposition of AI implementation.

Step 5: Hire the Right Personnel

Invest in hiring or training employees with the necessary skills and expertise to drive your AI initiatives forward. Look for individuals with experience in data science, machine learning, software development, and domain-specific knowledge relevant to your industry.

Step 6: Appreciate Small Beginnings

Start small and focus on quick wins to build momentum and demonstrate the value of AI to stakeholders. Begin with pilot projects or proofs-of-concept that address specific use cases and deliver tangible results.

Step 7: Carry Out the Integration of Data

Ensure that your data infrastructure is robust and capable of supporting AI applications. Cleanse and organize your data to make it accessible and usable for AI algorithms, and establish protocols for data governance and security.

Step 8: Include AI in Your Daily Tasks

Incorporate AI tools and solutions into your daily workflows and processes to familiarize employees with AI technologies and encourage adoption. Provide training and support to help employees use AI effectively in their roles.

Step 9: Integrate AI with Balance

Strike a balance between using AI to automate tasks and augmenting human capabilities, and ensure it complements rather than replaces human expertise. Be mindful of ethical considerations, privacy concerns, and potential biases in AI algorithms, and prioritize transparency and accountability in your AI initiatives.

Step 10: Reconsider Storage in Your AI Plan

Review your data storage infrastructure and consider how it can support the growing volume and complexity of data generated by AI applications. Explore options for scalable and flexible storage solutions that can accommodate the demands of AI-driven analytics and insights.

Wrap-Up

AI offers many benefits to businesses, and it is important to start by identifying specific challenges or opportunities that AI can address. Think about the areas of your business where AI could make a significant impact and how it could help you streamline processes, make more informed decisions, and unlock new possibilities for innovation. Envisioning the potential applications of AI in your business can better prepare you for the detailed strategies that will be discussed in later chapters. In the next chapter, we will look into the practical aspects of AI integration, starting with automation. Automation serves as the first practical step for many businesses in their AI integration process. We will explore how automation can be used to streamline workflows, reduce manual labor, and enhance overall productivity.

2. Automation

Today's business world is so fast-paced that the need for efficiency and productivity has never been greater. Companies are constantly seeking new ways to simplify their operations and gain a competitive edge. This is where automation comes in.

According to McKinsey, companies that have integrated automation reported saving an average of 40% in operational costs and increasing productivity by up to 25%. In 2022, Amazon's robotic handling system, Robin, sorted 1 billion packages, accounting for one-eighth of all orders delivered worldwide. Robots handle tasks like picking and packing, allowing human workers to take charge of quality control and the shipping process. This explains the significant impact of automation in the business world.

Automation is more than just a buzzword—it's a basic shift in how businesses operate. It allows you to achieve unprecedented levels of efficiency and productivity. Automation is efficient in easing workflows, reducing costs, and improving the overall quality of your products and services.

In this chapter, we will look into the key principles of automation, examining its role in enhancing operational efficiency and driving business growth. We will also explore how GenAI, with its advanced natural language processing capabilities, can be used to automate routine tasks so you can create time and resources for other important things.

Benefits of Automation

Automation refers to the use of technology to perform tasks with minimal human intervention. It involves the use of software, robots, and other technologies to automate processes and operations. The use of automation reduces the need for manual labor and increases efficiency.

Automation can range from simple tasks like email notifications and data entry to more complex processes like customer service interactions and manufacturing operations. Automating these tasks increases efficiency and reduces errors.

In recent years, advancements in artificial intelligence and machine learning have expanded the possibilities for automation. These technologies allow systems to learn from data, make decisions, and perform tasks that previously required human intelligence. As a result, businesses can automate even more complex processes and achieve higher levels of productivity. Let's look at the additional benefits of automation.

1. **Increased Productivity:** Automation can significantly increase productivity by allowing machines to perform repetitive tasks more quickly and accurately than humans. This allows your employees to work on other tasks that add value to your business, resulting in higher overall productivity levels.

2. **Stronger Security:** Automation enhances security measures by reducing the risk of human error, consistently applying access controls, monitoring unusual activity, and promptly responding to potential threats. Automated security protocols help safeguard sensitive data and protect against cyberattacks.

3. **Streamlined Compliance:** Compliance with regulations and standards is critical for businesses in many industries. Automation can help streamline compliance processes by ensuring that relevant rules and regulations are consistently applied and monitored, reducing the risk of noncompliance penalties.

4. **Greater Operational Efficiency:** Automation can lead to greater operational efficiency by reducing the time and resources required to complete tasks. This can result in cost savings and improved service delivery.

5. **Better Collaboration:** Automation facilitates better collaboration by providing employees with access to real-time data and insights. This can help teams work more effectively together to improve decision-making and outcomes within the company.

6. **Enhanced Service Delivery:** It helps businesses deliver faster, more efficient services to customers. Tasks that once required manual intervention can now be automated, with quicker response times and improved customer satisfaction.

7. **Significant Cost Savings:** One of the most significant benefits of automation is its ability to cut operational costs. Automating manual processes in businesses can save time and resources, minimize labor costs, and boost profitability.

8. **Reduced Errors:** Automation helps minimize the risk of errors that can occur during manual data entry or processing. With automation, your businesses can achieve greater accuracy and consistency in their operations. This leads to the production of higher-quality goods and services.

9. **Reliable Insights:** With automation, businesses can gather and analyze data more efficiently with valuable insights into customer behavior, market trends, and business performance. This can help businesses make better-informed decisions, improve overall performance, and stay ahead of the competition.

10. **Standardized Processes:** Automation helps standardize processes across an organization, ensuring consistency and efficiency. This can be particularly beneficial for businesses operating in multiple locations or dealing with large volumes of data. With automation, businesses can establish clear workflows and standard operating procedures to reduce variability and improve overall efficiency.

11. **Gained Transparency:** Organizations can track and monitor activities in real time, gaining insights into performance, resource allocation, and potential bottlenecks with automation. This increased transparency allows businesses to make informed decisions, note down areas for improvement, and optimize their operations for maximum efficiency.

12. **Heightened Morale:** Automation can enhance employee morale by eliminating repetitive tasks; this allows them to focus on more challenging work, resulting in greater job satisfaction and engagement. Also, automation reduces the likelihood of human error, boosting employees' confidence in their work.

How ChatGPT Integration Can Help with Automating Tasks

Artificial intelligence (AI) and natural language processing (NLP) have made it possible to create chatbots, which are computer programs that can have conversations with people and do certain tasks automatically.

One way to use ChatGPT is as a chatbot for customer support. It can answer frequently asked questions and handle many inquiries at once, which can save time and reduce the need for human support. Another application involves automating the creation of documents such as contracts or reports. This process relies on prompts and user-provided information. Using ChatGPT can minimize errors and facilitate the updating of templates to maintain document consistency. However, it may require additional training for optimal performance.

ChatGPT can also be used for language translation tasks. This AI tool is capable of translating large volumes of text in a short time, potentially reducing the dependence on human translators. Nonetheless, it may struggle to capture the nuanced meaning or cultural context of the original text.

Sentiment analysis is another valuable application of ChatGPT. It's adept at sorting extensive text datasets like customer feedback, with insights into customer sentiment and preferences. It can generate content tasks such as blog posts, social media posts, news articles, or product descriptions. It simplifies the content creation process and delivers content on time and consistently.

It can also function as a virtual assistant, helping with different administrative tasks like scheduling appointments to enhance efficiency and accessibility, as it is available round-the-clock. However, additional security measures may be needed to safeguard user data.

Hence, before automating with ChatGPT, you need to understand that certain tasks can and cannot be automated. Now, let's look at the step-by-step guide on how your business can identify tasks that are suitable for automation.

Step 1: Assess Your Current State

The first step is to evaluate your current business processes and look for areas where automation could be beneficial. Consider tasks that are repetitive, time-consuming, or prone to human error. Look for patterns in your workflows and pinpoint tasks that could be enhanced with automation.

Step 2: Define Your Automation Criteria

Next, establish clear criteria for determining which tasks are suitable for automation with AI. Consider factors such as the complexity of the task, frequency and volume of the task, the potential for automation using natural language processing, and the expected benefits in terms of efficiency, cost savings, or improved quality. Define what success looks like for each automated task.

Step 3: Prioritize Your Automation Opportunities

Once you have identified potential tasks for automation and defined your criteria, prioritize them based on their potential impact and feasibility. Assess the resources required for automation, the expected return on investment, and any dependencies or constraints that may affect implementation. You should focus on automating tasks that offer the greatest benefits with the least amount of effort.

Step 4: Choose Your Automation Tools

It's time to select the appropriate tools for implementation. ChatGPT's large language model is a tool that can be integrated into various automation platforms or used as a standalone solution. Factors such as ease of integration, scalability, and compatibility with your existing systems should influence your decision. Several automation platforms offer ChatGPT integration. Your business can opt to develop custom automation solutions using ChatGPT APIs for better flexibility and control over the automation process. This allows you to tailor solutions to your specific needs and requirements.

Step 5: Implement and Monitor Your Automation Solutions

To do this, set up ChatGPT within your chosen automation platform or integrate it into your existing systems. Depending on the complexity of the tasks being automated, this may involve configuring workflows, defining triggers, and setting up rules for ChatGPT interactions. If you are using ChatGPT in a customer service chatbot, you might use a platform like Dialogflow or Rasa to define the conversation flow, set triggers for specific responses, and establish rules for handling different types of inquiries. This involves designing the conversation logic, defining the actions ChatGPT should take based on user inputs, and ensuring that the chatbot responds appropriately to various scenarios.

Once implemented, you will need to monitor the performance of your automation solutions and make adjustments as needed. Track key metrics such as task completion times, error rates, and overall efficiency to evaluate the effectiveness of ChatGPT in automating tasks. You should also review regularly and optimize your automation workflows to ensure they remain aligned with your business goals and objectives.

Chatbots for Business Automation

ChatGPT, with its advanced natural language processing capabilities, is a valuable tool for automating various aspects of business operations beyond what you can imagine. Here are key areas where ChatGPT can be used for automation:

Customer Support and Service

Automating customer support processes is easy with chatbots. It does this by handling routine inquiries, providing 24/7 assistance, and resolving common issues. You can integrate ChatGPT into your website or messaging platforms to offer instant responses to customer queries, thereby improving response times.

To implement this, you would need to set up the ChatGPT system on your website or messaging platforms using an API or SDK provided by the platform hosting ChatGPT. Once integrated, ChatGPT can analyze incoming messages from customers in real time and generate instant responses based on the content of the messages and any predefined rules or knowledge bases you have set up. These responses will help address common customer queries, provide information about products or services, or offer assistance with specific tasks.

Content Creation

Many businesses use ChatGPT to generate content for marketing campaigns, industry trends, FAQs, blog posts, social media posts, product descriptions, and more. To do this, you need to provide ChatGPT with prompts or input data to generate content that aligns with their brand voice and messaging. A marketing agency can use ChatGPT to generate social media captions for their clients by inputting relevant information such as the client's industry, target audience, and key messages, while ChatGPT generates engaging captions tailored to each client's needs.

Employee Training and Onboarding

Employee onboarding software tools, such as BambooHR, Rippling, Talmundo, Happyfox, Capacity, etc., can assist your HR team in delivering a seamless onboarding experience for new hires. Businesses can create interactive training modules for new employees using AI. The training material can be developed by crafting detailed scripts that cover various aspects of the onboarding process and employee training. These scripts may include common questions, step-by-step guides, simulations of real-world scenarios, etc.

AI can then be integrated into the training platform, allowing employees to interact with it just like they would with a human trainer. Employees can ask questions, seek clarification, and receive guidance tailored to their needs and progress. It can also provide instant feedback on the completion of tasks, quiz responses, or simulations to help employees learn from their mistakes and improve their skills.

Automated Scheduling

Scheduling appointments, interviews, meetings, and events can be time-consuming; you could divert such time into doing other things or simply taking a break. Although ChatGPT does not have the capability to schedule appointments directly, you would need to integrate the Zapier ChatGPT plugin with a scheduling tool or platform like Motion, TARS, ArtiBot.ai, etc., that can handle appointment bookings.

For instance, you can use the ChatGPT-powered chatbot to understand appointment preferences such as date, time, or type of appointment, and then you can use this information to schedule the appointment through the integrated scheduling system. The chatbot could also provide you with confirmation details once the appointment is successfully booked. This automation reduces the need for manual scheduling.

Summary and Outline Writing

After a hectic meeting and long day, ChatGPT can help automate the creation of summaries and outlines for documents, reports, or presentations. You can use ChatGPT to automatically summarize lengthy documents or draft outlines based on key points or themes. For instance, your marketing team can use ChatGPT to summarize customer feedback from surveys or create outlines for upcoming blog posts or marketing campaigns.

Responsive Chatbots

ChatGPT can be used to create responsive chatbots that are capable of interacting with customers and providing information or assistance. To create responsive chatbots, you need to collect relevant data such as FAQs, product information, and troubleshooting guides to teach ChatGPT how to generate appropriate responses. Once trained, ChatGPT can then be integrated into a chatbot platform or messaging app to provide support for common customer service issues. ChatGPT's natural language processing capabilities allow it to understand and respond to customer queries in a human-like manner, improving the overall customer experience.

Market Research

ChatGPT is effective in streamlining market research efforts by automating tasks such as data collection, analysis, and report generation. Your business can use AI to scour online forums, social media platforms, and customer feedback channels to gather insights on consumer preferences, trends, and sentiment. This is done by crafting personalized review request messages you can send to your customers and analyzing them using ChatGPT natural language processing (NLP) algorithms to understand the sentiment, extract key topics, and identify common trends. This analysis helps businesses gauge customer satisfaction, pinpoint areas for improvement, and make informed decisions based on customer feedback.

For instance, a cosmetics company that wants to understand consumer preferences for skincare products can use ChatGPT to craft customers' review requests so as to collect and analyze these reviews. ChatGPT then identifies recurring keywords and themes, such as "anti-aging," "moisturizing," and "natural ingredients," indicating high consumer demand for these features. Based on this analysis, the company develops a new line of skincare products tailored to meet these preferences, resulting in increased sales and customer satisfaction.

Data Analysis and Reporting

Data analysis and reporting tasks become less stressful with ChatGPT. It extracts actionable information from large datasets quickly and efficiently. ChatGPT can process financial data, sales figures, or customer surveys to generate reports, charts, and graphs summarizing key findings and trends.

A retail chain can analyze sales data to identify top-performing products and optimize inventory management using ChatGPT. It analyzes sales figures from different store locations, identifies trends, and generates a comprehensive report highlighting best-selling products, sales trends, and customer demographics. This helps the company adjust its inventory levels and improve store layouts to maximize sales.

Social Media Management

ChatGPT can help in managing social media presence by automating tasks such as content creation, scheduling posts, and responding to customer inquiries. For instance, businesses can use ChatGPT to generate engaging social media posts, write product descriptions, or draft responses to customer comments and messages. It can also schedule posts with tools like UpGrow, Flick, Content Studio, etc., at optimal times, monitor engagement metrics, and respond to customer queries in real time. This automation helps you maintain a consistent and active presence on social media platforms and drive engagement to build customer relationships.

Prompts for Business Automation

Here are practical examples of prompts you can feed ChatGPT to help you generate reports, manage emails, and schedule meetings. Be sure to give ChatGPT relevant information about your business, including any specific requirements, preferences, or constraints that need to be considered when automating the task.

Generating Reports

- Create a comprehensive customer segmentation report based on demographic data, purchase history, and behavioral patterns, identifying key customer segments and their preferences.
- Produce a market research report on emerging trends and opportunities in the healthcare industry, focusing on advancements in medical technology, regulatory changes, and consumer demand.
- Generate a financial performance report for the current fiscal year, analyzing key metrics such as revenue growth, profit margins, and operating expenses and providing insights into financial health and stability.
- Provide an inventory management report detailing current stock levels, inventory turnover rates, and stockout occurrences, and offer recommendations for optimizing inventory levels and reducing carrying costs.
- Produce a marketing campaign performance report, evaluating the effectiveness of recent marketing initiatives, such as email campaigns, PPC advertising, and social media promotions, and measuring ROI and conversion rates.
- Create a website traffic analysis report, summarizing website traffic patterns, user behavior, and conversion metrics and identifying opportunities for improving website performance and user experience.
- Provide a supply chain efficiency report, analyzing supply chain processes, lead times, and inventory

turnover ratios and recommending strategies for reducing costs and improving operational efficiency.

- Produce a customer churn analysis report, analyzing churn rates, reasons for customer attrition, and customer retention strategies and providing recommendations for reducing churn and improving customer loyalty.
- Provide a risk management report, identifying potential risks and vulnerabilities, assessing their potential impact on business operations, and outlining risk mitigation strategies and contingency plans.

Managing Emails

- Create a follow-up email for a sales lead, expressing appreciation for their interest in your products or services and offering additional information or assistance to facilitate the sales process.
- Write a response to a customer complaint or negative feedback, acknowledging their concerns, apologizing for any inconvenience, and outlining steps taken to address the issue and ensure customer satisfaction.
- Draft an email announcement for an upcoming product launch or promotion, highlighting key features, benefits, and promotional offers and encouraging recipients to take advantage of the opportunity.
- Create a thank-you email for a recent purchase, expressing gratitude for the customer's business, providing order details, and inviting feedback or suggestions for improvement.

- Write a response to a partnership inquiry or collaboration proposal, expressing interest in the opportunity, outlining potential benefits and synergies, and proposing the next steps for further discussion.
- Draft an email newsletter for subscribers featuring company updates, product announcements, industry insights, and relevant content to engage and inform recipients and encourage continued interaction with your brand.
- Write a response to a job application or inquiry, thanking the applicant for their interest, providing information on the hiring process, and requesting any additional materials or information needed for consideration.
- Draft an email announcement for a company policy update or procedural change, clearly communicating the changes, the reasons behind them, and any actions employees need to take to comply with the new policies.
- Write a reminder email for an upcoming deadline or important meeting, providing details on the event, any required preparations, and a friendly reminder to ensure attendance or completion of tasks.
- Create an email outreach campaign for prospecting or lead generation, introducing your company or services, highlighting key benefits or features, and inviting recipients to learn more or schedule a consultation.

Schedule Planning

With the Zapier ChatGPT plugin, you can integrate ChatGPT with over 5,000 compatible apps. This means you can direct ChatGPT to perform tasks in other apps, like scheduling meetings in Google Calendar or updating spreadsheets in Notion. Let's look at some ChatGPT prompts that can help you schedule planning:

- Can you help me prioritize my tasks this week/month? I need to do the following: (Provide your to-do list).
- Create a project plan for implementing a remote work policy detailing communication strategies, technology requirements, and employee training.
- Develop strategies to ensure successful project delivery and minimize the risk associated with (type of project).
- Develop a timeline template for (type of project) that can be easily adjusted to accommodate changing requirements.
- I need tips on effective team collaboration and communication during marketing campaigns to ensure all team members are on the same page.
- Create a project plan for (type of project) that will help me stay organized at work.
- Develop strategies for tracking progress on (type of project) to ensure deadlines are met and expectations are exceeded.
- Devise a strategy for communicating project progress and updates to stakeholders and team members on (type of project) to maintain transparency.

Wrap-Up

In business automation, it's important to look ahead and far beyond operational efficiency and consider the impact it can have on customer support and overall customer experience. Customer support is easier with chatbots, as they offer opportunities to provide instant, personalized assistance to customers around the clock—from answering common questions to resolving issues and processing transactions—while reducing wait times and improving response times. The next chapter will be an eye-opener into the wonders of chatbots and explore how they can ease customer support operations and elevate customer experience to new heights.

3. Customer Support

Businesses are constantly looking for ways to improve their customer support services and deliver exceptional experiences to their customers. One notable solution that has emerged in recent years is the use of chatbots. These AI-driven bots have significantly changed customer support services with unparalleled 24/7 assistance and enhanced customer satisfaction.

Did you know that businesses implementing chatbots have seen a significant improvement in customer satisfaction? According to Uberall, 80% of customers who interact with an AI chatbot say they have a positive experience, explaining the growing importance of AI-driven chatbots in delivering top-notch customer support.

With chatbots, customers can get instant answers to their queries, any time of day or night, without having to wait in long queues or walk through complex phone menus. It promises a seamless and efficient customer support experience that meets the needs of today's on-demand consumers.

However, in this chapter, we will discuss the huge impact that chatbots can have on customer support in your business. We will guide you through integrating AI into your customer service framework, exploring the benefits, challenges, and best practices for implementing chatbots effectively.

The Transformation with Chatbots

For almost every website you visit, you get a "Hi, this is Adriana. How can I help you today?" and it's interesting to know that you get an instant response like you are chatting in real life with customer support personnel about your concern. It wasn't like this many years ago, as you had to wait for human response, which can take more time and require more customer service personnel working shifts—extra costs for the company. Who would have thought that customer service could be automated? But here we have it, changing our business world.

One of the main jobs of chatbots is to handle common questions that customers often ask. They do this by finding the right answers from the information available to them. This is super handy because it means that customers can get help in no time without having to wait for a human to respond. Rather than your workers providing similar answers to the same questions from customers all the time, they can handle more complicated issues that need human attention in the organization.

Another interesting thing about these chatbots is that they can make it seem like you are talking to a real person. They are trained to understand different types of questions and respond in a friendly and helpful way. So, even though you are chatting with a machine, it feels like you are chatting with a human.

Now, let's look at the numerous advantages of integrating chatbots into your business.

Fast, 24/7 Customer Service

Chatbots offer lightning-fast responses to customer inquiries. These chatbots can instantly assist round-the-clock, ensuring that customers receive help whenever they need it, regardless of time zones or business hours. This quick response time enhances customer satisfaction by addressing issues promptly, reducing wait times, and preventing frustration.

More Personalized Experiences

AI-powered support systems can deliver personalized experiences to each customer. It analyzes customer data and interaction history and then tailors responses to suit individual preferences and needs. This personalization creates a more engaging and meaningful customer experience, increasing customer loyalty and driving repeat business. Also, AI support systems can remember past interactions with customers, allowing for continuity and consistency in service, which further enhances customer experience and relationships.

Deliver Multilingual Support

With AI-powered support systems, your business can communicate with customers in multiple languages. This capability breaks down language barriers and ensures that your business can effectively serve customers from diverse language backgrounds. Whether it's answering questions in Chinese, German, Italian, English, Arab, and many more—just name it—or providing product information or resolving issues, AI can do so in the customer's preferred language. This enhances the accessibility of support services and expands the reach of businesses to a global audience.

Ensure More Consistent Support

One of the key advantages of AI-powered support is its ability to provide consistent assistance to customers. Unlike human agents, who may vary in their responses due to factors like mood, fatigue, or knowledge level, AI-powered systems deliver consistent and standardized support every time. This ensures that all customers receive the same level of service quality, regardless of when they reach out for assistance. Consistency in support leads to increased customer satisfaction, as businesses can rely on AI to consistently meet customers' needs and expectations.

Convenient Self-Service Options

With chatbots, you can respond quickly and accurately to common inquiries by providing relevant information and assisting your customers with basic tasks, all without the need for human intervention. This means that customers can get help whenever they need it without having to wait for a human agent to be available. This allows customers to find solutions on their terms, whether it's checking account balances, tracking orders, or troubleshooting issues, improving their overall experience with the brand.

Proactive Customer Service

AI-powered support systems allow businesses to provide proactive customer service by anticipating and addressing customer needs before they even arise. Through predictive analytics and machine learning algorithms, these systems can use customer data and behavior patterns to check for potential issues or opportunities for engagement. For instance, if a customer frequently buys a specific product, the system might proactively offer information about related products or provide tips on how to use the product effectively. This proactive approach helps businesses anticipate and resolve customer problems more effectively and build trust and loyalty in customers.

Delivering Omnichannel Support

Chatbots break the barrier that customers face with having to use different channels of communication to voice their complaints or reach out to your business. AI-powered chatbots provide seamless support across multiple channels, such as chat, email, phone, and social media. This allows customers to reach out for help through their preferred communication channel, making it more convenient for them to get assistance.

Also, AI-powered systems can maintain context across channels, ensuring a consistent and personalized experience for customers regardless of how they choose to interact with the business. This omnichannel approach improves customer satisfaction and builds loyalty by providing a cohesive and streamlined support experience.

Improving Service with Every Interaction

AI-powered support systems are capable of learning and improving over time through machine learning algorithms. However, you need to feed the AI system with a large amount of customer data. This includes past interactions like chats, emails, and even voice recordings. The AI can learn to identify patterns in customer inquiries, categorize issues, and match them with the most appropriate responses by analyzing the data using machine learning algorithms.

With a feedback loop, customers can rate the helpfulness of the AI's response, allowing the system to learn from its mistakes and improve over time. Also, human experts should be involved in reviewing AI responses and refining the data used for training to ensure that it stays accurate and addresses evolving customer needs.

Continuously improving its capabilities can enhance the overall quality of service and deliver more personalized and effective support to customers. This helps your business optimize support processes and drive operational efficiency.

Collect Customer Feedback

AI can efficiently collect and analyze customer feedback, which provides your business with insights into customer preferences, satisfaction levels, and pain points. AI uses a mix of direct and indirect methods to collect customer feedback. On the direct side, it might ask to rate their helpfulness with a thumbs up/down or a star system. You can also add short surveys to the AI algorithm after an interaction to gauge customers' experiences.

On the flipside, AI can analyze language in chats or emails to help understand customers' sentiments—happy, frustrated, or somewhere in between. This allows businesses to identify trends, prioritize areas for improvement, and make informed decisions to enhance the overall customer experience.

Reduce Customer Requests

It can help reduce the volume of customer requests by providing self-service options and automating routine tasks. AI chatbots offer instant answers to common inquiries, guide customers through simple processes, such as account updates or order tracking, and deflect a significant number of requests that would otherwise require human intervention. Incorporating AI chatbots into your business operation increases efficiency and reduces operational costs.

Integrating AI Agents for 24/7 Support

Integrating ChatGPT chatbots into existing customer support channels can be a strategic move to improve customer service and your business as a whole. Here's a step-by-step guide to help you through the process:

Step 1: Choose Your Data Type

First, determine the type of data you want your chatbot to access and respond to. This could include FAQs, product information, troubleshooting guides, or any other relevant data that customers might inquire about.

Step 2: Using Website URLs

One way to integrate ChatGPT chatbots into your customer support channels is by providing access to specific website URLs. This allows the chatbot to crawl through your website's content and extract relevant information to answer customer queries. Ensure that the URLs provided contain up-to-date and accurate information.

Step 3: Using Single Links

Alternatively, you can provide single links to specific resources or documents that contain the information your chatbot needs to respond to customer inquiries. This method is useful for accessing resources such as PDF manuals, knowledge base articles, or support documentation.

Step 4: Using Sitemap Data

The next step is to use sitemap data to train your chatbot. Sitemaps provide a structured overview of your website's content, making it easier for the chatbot to navigate and access relevant information. Integrating sitemap data into your chatbot's training process helps ensure easy access to a comprehensive repository of information to assist customers effectively.

Step 5: Training the Chatbot

Once you have determined the data type and access method for your chatbot, it's time to train it. Use machine learning techniques to train your chatbot on the specific data sources and information relevant to your business. This may involve providing examples of questions and corresponding answers, refining responses based on feedback, and continuously updating and improving the chatbot's knowledge base.

Step 6: Adding Bot Details

To do this, start by defining the purpose and scope of your ChatGPT chatbot. Determine the specific tasks and inquiries it will handle, such as answering FAQs, providing product information, or assisting with troubleshooting. Then, customize the bot's name, avatar, and tone to align with your brand identity and customer preferences.

Step 7: Editing and Adding More Knowledge

Continuously update and refine your chatbot by editing existing responses and adding new knowledge based on user feedback and evolving customer needs. You should also regularly review chat transcripts and analytics to identify areas for improvement.

Step 8: Retraining the Chatbot

The next step is to periodically review and retrain your ChatGPT chatbot to keep it up-to-date with the latest information and customer inquiries. Analyze your customer interactions and feedback to check for ways you can improve or new topics to add. Then, use this feedback to refine the bot's responses, adjust its training data, and enhance its conversational abilities.

Step 9: Testing Your Chatbot

Before deploying your ChatGPT chatbot to live customer support channels, thoroughly test its functionality and performance. Conduct various test scenarios to ensure that the bot accurately understands user queries and provides relevant responses. You can test for different use cases, language variations, and edge cases to discover any potential issues or limitations in the future. Make necessary adjustments and iterations based on test results to optimize the bot's performance.

Step 10: Further Learning

Continuous learning is essential for maximizing the effectiveness of your ChatGPT chatbot. Monitor its interactions with customers in real time and gather feedback from users to spot areas for improvement. Focus on analyzing chat transcripts, user ratings, and customer satisfaction metrics to measure the bot's performance and identify opportunities for further learning and refinement.

Look for patterns where the chatbot stumbles. Are there frequent misunderstandings of user queries? Are conversations going off track? Are specific keywords tripping the bot up? Are there repeated questions? Is a negative tone emerging as the conversation progresses? Does the conversation feel natural or clunky? Are there opportunities for the chatbot to offer more information or make proactive suggestions to enhance the user experience? Analyzing the flow of conversation helps identify areas where the chatbot can be more helpful and engaging. Use this feedback to enhance the bot's knowledge base, refine its conversational abilities, and improve overall customer satisfaction.

Although ChatGPT chatbots have a lot of benefits when integrated into your business operation, you might, however, have to face certain challenges in their integration process. Knowing these challenges ahead can help you stay prepared and ahead of your game. Below are potential challenges you should expect and ways to overcome them:

Natural Language Understanding

One of the primary challenges businesses may face is ensuring that the chatbot can accurately understand and interpret user queries, especially when they are phrased in natural language. The chatbot may struggle with understanding different phrasings, slang, or misspelled words, which can result in inaccurate or irrelevant responses.

To overcome this challenge, you can invest in training the chatbot with a diverse range of training data and examples to improve its natural language understanding. Also, using prebuilt models and frameworks for natural language processing can help enhance the chatbot's ability to comprehend user inputs accurately.

Domain Knowledge and Training Data

Integrating AI chatbots into customer support systems may pose a problem due to the need for extensive training data. Sourcing for sufficient domain knowledge and training data to provide relevant and accurate responses to user queries, particularly in specialized or niche industries, can be time-consuming and resource-intensive.

You can address this by regularly curating and updating the chatbot's training data to reflect the latest trends and developments in their industry. Integrate your chatbot with external knowledge bases and resources to supplement its domain knowledge and leverage transfer learning techniques to generalize its knowledge from one domain to another, improving its overall effectiveness.

User Experience and Personalization

Ensuring a seamless user experience and personalized interactions can be challenging when integrating ChatGPT chatbots. Customers expect chatbots to understand their queries accurately and provide relevant responses tailored to their needs. However, without proper customization and personalization, the chatbot may struggle to meet these expectations.

To solve this hurdle, businesses can customize the chatbot's responses based on user data and behavior. Implementing user profiling and context awareness can help the chatbot deliver more personalized interactions. Also, providing options for users to escalate to human agents when needed can enhance the user experience.

Integration with Existing Systems

You may struggle with integrating ChatGPT chatbots with existing systems and platforms in your business's infrastructure. Your businesses may encounter compatibility issues, data silos, and technical complexities when trying to connect the chatbot with CRM systems, databases, and other backend systems.

Businesses can overcome this challenge by selecting chatbot platforms that offer seamless integration with existing systems through APIs and connectors called webhooks. Prioritize compatibility and data consistency between systems to ensure smooth operation. Consider working closely with IT and development teams to help address any technical issues that arise during integration.

Enhancing Customer Satisfaction with AI

Customer service plays a pivotal role in determining business success. To improve customer satisfaction using ChatGPT chatbots, businesses can employ several strategies that include the following:

Provide 24/7 Support

Use ChatGPT chatbots to provide round-the-clock support to your customers, ensuring that they can receive assistance anytime, even during holidays or nonbusiness hours. For instance, as a travel agency, you can integrate chatbots into your business's website to help customers book flights and hotels. The chatbot operates 24/7, allowing customers to make reservations or inquire about travel plans at any time. This availability enhances customer satisfaction by providing timely responses to queries and issues.

Instant Issue Resolution

With the speed and efficiency of chatbots, your business can attend to customers' inquiries and provide quick resolutions to their issues. Integrating chatbots can assist customers with product inquiries and order tracking. Visitors can receive immediate responses to their questions, such as product availability or delivery status, improving their overall shopping experience.

Cost-Effective Solution

Opt for ChatGPT chatbots as a cost-effective alternative to hiring, training, and managing human customer support agents. Your small business can use a chatbot on its website to handle customer inquiries and support requests. This can help save on staffing costs while still providing efficient and responsive customer service.

Integration with Live Chat

Combining live chat with chatbots allows businesses to offer a hybrid support solution. Customers can interact with a live agent when needed while still benefiting from the efficiency of chatbots. Customers have the option to make simple inquiries with chatbots or escalate issues to a live agent for more complex issues to ensure personalized assistance.

Personalized Recommendations

With the intelligence of ChatGPT chatbots, you can study customer preferences and provide personalized product recommendations or assistance. For example, an online fashion store can use a chatbot to interact with customers and gather information about their preferences and past purchases. The chatbot will use the data to suggest relevant products and offer personalized shopping assistance for customers.

Transcript Analysis

Data and transcripts from chatbot conversations are useful in helping businesses gain valuable insights into customer preferences, behaviors, and pain points. A clothing business can implement chatbots to analyze transcripts to identify common customer issues and improve its services and delivery.

Prompts for Customer Service

Here are a few ChatGPT prompts for customer service. These prompts combine direct instructions with hypothetical situations to guide customer service personnel on how to address various issues customers may encounter using ChatGPT:

- As a customer service representative at (your company name), imagine dealing with an irate customer. Respond by acknowledging their frustration and expressing empathy. Assure them that you are there to help resolve their issue and provide a positive experience.
- Generate a script to engage with a potential customer who is curious about your products/services. Introduce yourself warmly, express gratitude for your interest, and offer helpful information about your offerings without being pushy.
- As a customer service agent for (company name), you will be addressing an issue with our (software product) that causes it to crash upon opening. Many customers are unable to use the product, and some are seeking

refunds. Draft a response to empathize with their frustrations and politely request their patience as our team works on a fix.

- A customer is curious about our product and wants to know how it stands out from similar products in the market. Respond as a knowledgeable customer service agent and provide the customer with relevant information about our product (product name), highlighting its unique features and benefits (provide ChatGPT with its key features and benefits).

- We offer fixed packages with fixed pricing, but a customer wants to customize their package to suit their needs. Respond as a customer-centric service provider and offer to accommodate their request within reason, as we occasionally allow for personalization on special requests.

- Craft an email to express appreciation for a customer's business or purchase and reiterate the company's commitment to providing excellent service.

- Draft a response to acknowledge customers' wait times, offer an estimated wait, and suggest alternative solutions like browsing self-help resources while they wait.

- Our website is experiencing technical glitches, causing issues with order placement, viewing recent orders, and tracking order status. Provide three variations of empathetic scripts to handle customer queries regarding the issue with patience and understanding.

- A customer seeks assistance in understanding the technical process behind our software (name of software). Summarize a knowledge base article to provide step-by-step instructions you can use to guide customers through the process (provide ChatGPT with the article).

- Craft a response when a customer inquires about a product you cannot access information about due to department specialization (e.g., tech support for a clothing store).
- Develop a polite and clear script to direct customers to our self-help knowledge base and chatbot to resolve generic queries and issues efficiently.

Wrap-Up

In conclusion, the advancements in AI-powered customer support have changed the way businesses interact with their customers and improved the customer experience. The e-commerce sector, in particular, has benefited greatly from these advancements, resulting in more personalized and seamless shopping experiences for consumers. In the next chapter, we will look into how AI and ChatGPT are transforming the e-commerce sector, creating tailored shopping experiences that cater to individual preferences and needs. From personalized product recommendations to intelligent virtual assistants, the potential applications of AI in e-commerce are vast and promising. Stay glued as we explore the future of online shopping powered by AI.

4. E-Commerce

The digital world is vastly advancing, and companies/organizations are ready to utilize this technology to their advantage to make customer experience the highlight among their competitors. E-commerce is one of the major areas that has undergone tremendous technological advancement. The creation of language processing technology has enabled organizations and companies to offer incredibly individualized and effective customer service.

ChatGPT is one technological advancement that is topping the list. According to Twinkle, businesses implementing AI have seen an average increase of 35% in customer conversion rates. It has a human language working ability and is built on crafting and comprehending meaningful and relevant texts. This makes it an excellent tool for building human-like relationships with clients in e-commerce. This and more are promises of AI in e-commerce.

In this chapter, we will explore the various ways AI, particularly ChatGPT, is being used in the e-commerce sector. We will look at case studies, industry trends, and practical applications to unveil the power of AI in creating seamless shopping experiences online.

Personalized Shopping Experience with ChatGPT

Personalization in e-commerce deals with tailoring individuals' online shopping experiences to their preferences. This can be done through targeted marketing messages, customized website interfaces, and recommending personalized products based on the client's browsing history. The motive is to improve user satisfaction and drive conversions by rendering useful content to each shopper.

Natural language processing (NLP) is important in achieving personalization in e-commerce. By clarifying customers' language and desires, e-commerce companies can deliver a more personalized experience that meets customers' expectations. Also, customer feedback, comments, or reviews by NLP can help e-commerce companies make better recommendations to customers.

This can be done by overviewing the client's purchasing history and suggesting goods and services that agree with the customer's preferences. This is a win-win for both customers and businesses, as companies are able to deliver an authentic experience to each customer, which will, in turn, build trust and loyalty while customers get excess value for their money.

Future Applications of AI in E-Commerce

In the coming years, the use of AI in e-commerce will go beyond creating optimized content for your business website. You should be prepared to embrace the soon-to-be transformation that will happen with AI in a few years' time. However, here's a glimpse into some exciting potential applications of AI that will reshape the online shopping experience:

- **Pricing Optimization:** AI will be more effective in analyzing market trends, competitor pricing, demand forecasting, and customer behavior to optimize pricing strategies. This will help e-commerce businesses maximize revenue, increase competitiveness, and capitalize on market opportunities.
- **Hyper-Personalization:** AI will go beyond simple product recommendations. In the future, it can act as a virtual stylist, suggesting outfits based on customers' preferences, body types, and even weather conditions by analyzing customers' past purchases, browsing history, and social media activity to create an individualized shopping experience.
- **Voice Search Revolution:** With AI advancements, voice search will become a dominant force in e-commerce. Customers will be able to seamlessly search for products and complete purchases using just their voice. This will be transformative for mobile shopping and hands-free interactions, especially for busy customers.
- **AI-Powered Logistics and Delivery:** AI can streamline logistics by optimizing delivery routes, predicting

potential delays, and enabling autonomous delivery vehicles. This will lead to faster deliveries, reduced costs, and a more transparent delivery experience for customers.

- **Visual Search and Personalized Recommendations:** AI will be able to power advanced image recognition, allowing customers to search for products using images or even by taking a picture of an item they like. This will further personalize product recommendations and bridge the gap between physical and online shopping experiences.

- **Augmented Reality (AR) and Virtual Try-On:** AI will integrate with AR and virtual try-on technology to allow customers to visualize products in their environment, try on virtual clothing or accessories, and make more informed purchase decisions.

As technology keeps evolving, we are expecting to see more interesting applications of AI in the e-commerce industry.

How to Integrate ChatGPT for E-commerce Website

Integrating ChatGPT with e-commerce platforms can significantly improve your customer shopping experience by providing personalized product recommendations and offers. Here are the steps to incorporating ChatGPT into your e-commerce business:

Select a Chatbot Platform

Begin by choosing a platform or service that provides a chatbot or conversational AI powered by GPT. Examples of such platforms include Giosg, Chatfuel, Flow XO, etc. These platforms offer tools and APIs for building and deploying your chatbot.

Plan Conversation Flow

Design the flow of conversation for your chatbot. Consider the various features and functionalities you want your chatbot to offer. This could include providing product information, assisting with order tracking, personalized recommendations, answering FAQs, and more.

Develop Chatbot Responses

The next step is to develop possible questions, answers, and responses to help train your chatbot for better performance. Ensure that the responses are structured and tailored to your target audience. Depending on the type of platform you choose, it will provide guidelines on how to prepare and format the data for training your chatbot.

Integrate with Your Webshop

After training your chatbot, the next step is to integrate it with your webshop. This involves embedding the chatbot interface or incorporating JavaScript codes into your website so that customers can easily access this feature while browsing products on your website.

1. **Test and Refine**: Before launching your chatbot, thoroughly test it to ensure that it functions correctly and provides the right responses when prompted. Gather feedback from test users, and use this feedback to refine and improve your chatbot's performance.

2. **Launch and Monitor**: Once you are satisfied with your chatbot's performance, launch it on your webshop. Monitor its performance closely and make adjustments as necessary to enhance its effectiveness.

3. **Continuously Improve**: Regularly review and analyze your chatbot's interactions with customers. Use this data to identify areas for improvement and make updates to your chatbot to enhance its capabilities and improve the overall shopping experience for your customers.

Inventory Management Optimization

AI is useful in inventory management in a good number of ways. Integrating AI into your inventory management system helps to monitor stock levels in real time, send notifications when inventory levels are low, and suggest when to place new orders with suppliers.

With AI, it becomes easier to sort and process useful historical data, current inventory levels, and market trends to forecast demand and optimize inventory levels. This proactive approach helps reduce stockouts, minimize excess inventory, and improve overall inventory turnover rates. Also, it streamlines inventory management tasks by automating routine processes such as order processing, inventory tracking, and supplier communication. This automation saves time and reduces the risk of human error. Some of the best AI-powered inventory management software solutions include Fishbowl, SkuVault, Zoho Inventory, etc.

Now, let's look at more ways artificial intelligence optimizes your inventory:

1. **Scheduling Production Runs:** AI has the ability to analyze sales data and customer demand to figure out the product that will be in high demand and use the findings to plan production affairs in a way that limits waste and maximizes efficiency. It can provide concrete information about market trends and patterns, pricing systems, and product quality, directing the course of the decision process in the company.
2. **Monitoring Inventory Levels:** Your business can adopt AI with a manufacturer's inventory management system to track stock levels in real time. Notifications will be sent at low inventory levels, showing recommendations for when to place orders for new products from suppliers. Users can monitor cost and performance easily.
3. **Coordinating with Suppliers:** Distribution of delivery processes can be done with AI from suppliers to

producers and vice versa. Items can be selected, and the selection of the right route, including transportation costs, can be optimized. Automated information will be sent to confirm delivery time and quantity while providing accurate updates on inventory levels and production time. In optimizing inventory management with AI, it is important to use accurate and comprehensive tags and descriptions; these tags should be properly categorized. It helps quicken data analysis and facilitation.

Leveraging Customer Data for Smart Decisions

ChatGPT's role in analyzing customer data for smart decisions is multifaceted and impactful. Its natural language processing (NLP) and deep learning capabilities allow it to process vast amounts of unstructured customer data, such as reviews, feedback, and interactions, to extract valuable insights.

ChatGPT's human-like manner of understanding is what makes it stand out among other AI technologies in the market. Customers do not have to repeatedly submit their problems for the system to understand. It provides loads of benefits in customer service as it uses natural and familiar words to interact with its users—including sarcasm and humor. Customers derive more satisfaction when they "feel" like they are interacting with a person who is interested in solving their problem rather than a robot.

Also, AI tools can analyze customer behavior patterns to predict future trends and anticipate customer needs. To do this, you need to gather customer data. This isn't just about purchases but also browsing habits, time spent on your site, and even social media interactions. By collecting this data and cleaning it up, you can feed it into AI models.

These AI models are like smart machines that learn from the data. Some recommend products based on past purchases (think "Customers who bought this, also bought …"), while others identify groups of customers with similar behavior for targeted marketing campaigns. There are even models that predict future actions, like when a customer might buy something or what they are interested in.

Once the AI is trained, it's time to put it to work. You integrate it with different parts of your business, like your website, app, or email marketing. This allows the AI to personalize the customer experience in real time. You also constantly monitor how the AI performs, seeing if customers click on recommendations or if they are happy with the experience. This new data is fed back into the AI, keeping it up-to-date and improving its ability to predict customer needs.

Prompts for E-commerce

Below are some interesting ChatGPT prompts you can try out on your own:

- **Prompt for creating engaging product titles**: Create seven attractive and persuasive product titles for mini electronic hand fans.

- **Prompt for building e-commerce landing pages**: Create a compelling landing page for our new product line of sustainable fashion accessories. Focus on key selling points such as eco-friendly materials, unique designs, and social impact. The landing page must be persuasive and include clear calls-to-action.
- **Prompt for e-commerce social media content ideas**: Brainstorm creative social media content ideas for our e-commerce fashion brand, targeting young adults, incorporating trending fashion topics, styling tips, and user-generated content.
- **Prompt for e-commerce email campaign ideas**: Create an email campaign that targets personalized recommendations and new product promotions for a virtual kitchen utensil store.
- **Prompt for e-commerce product launch strategies**: Create a product launch plan that focuses on targeting influencers, adopting marketing mediums, and monitoring the performance of launch campaigns for a new model of smartphone device.
- **Prompt for e-commerce FAQ**: Create a list of FAQs and provide accurate answers for an upcoming social media application launch.
- **Prompt for e-commerce online shopping payment method:** Come up with five payment method ideas that are accessible and easy to navigate for digital book purchases in an online bookshop.
- **Prompt for e-commerce advertisement**: Design three major templates that contain quality, appealing, and

compelling video, image, and written content for an interior decoration brand.

- **Prompt for e-commerce homepage content**: Create informative and exciting homepage content on a blog that deals with international travel experiences. Include pictures and theme designs.
- **Prompt for e-commerce sales boost**: Write an intriguing product description for a company that sells creamy yogurt with quality traits and health benefits, persuading a potential customer to make a purchase.
- **Prompt for e-commerce value showcase and cost-effectiveness:** Write a compelling product description for a premium light bulb, highlighting its top-tier features. Mention that the product includes free delivery and is available at a discounted price without disclosing the original price.
- **Prompt for e-commerce title optimization for search engines**: Generate sample titles for an agricultural product company specializing in organic fertilizers, ensuring optimization for ranking on various search engines. The titles should include relevant keywords related to organic farming, soil health, and sustainable agriculture practices.
- **Prompt for e-commerce Meta descriptions to deploy scarcity and urgency**: Create meta description content for fashion houses that focus on only corporate wear, indicating the urgency for limited stock available for purchase.
- **Prompt to identify e-commerce market opportunities**: Analyze the latest market trends and

consumer demand to recognize potential opportunities for growth in the e-commerce market.

- **Prompt for e-commerce sales funnel**: Highlight a constructive e-commerce sales funnel for optimization and create awareness for sales and maximum conversions.
- **Prompt for e-commerce customer segmentation ideas:** Suggest seven factors to segment customers to target marketing and effectively improve customer satisfaction.
- **Prompt for e-commerce user-generated content ideas:** Motivate customers to create and share reviews and media posts featuring the company's product.
- **Prompt for e-commerce blogging ideas:** Propose engaging and educative content ideas for a blog to attract traffic and educate potential customers.
- **Prompt for seasonal campaign planning:** Develop a seasonal marketing campaign for our outdoor apparel collection. Include ideas for social media content, email newsletters, and promotional offers.
- **Prompt for e-commerce customer survey questions**: Get customer feedback through targeted surveys that identify dissatisfaction and reveal opportunities for improvement.

Wrap-Up

There is a whole lot more in this book as we continue to explore different business sectors where AI and ChatGPT are game-changers. Having seen the booming effects of AI on e-commerce, it's evident that AI is reshaping not just online shopping but also customer engagement. The next chapter will look into content creation and marketing, explaining how AI enriches customer interactions with personalized content in your business.

5. Content Creation

If you have ever found yourself stuck trying to come up with engaging content for your social media page or struggling to brainstorm ideas for your next newsletter, you are not alone. Coming up with fresh and creative content ideas can be a challenge, especially when you are pressed for time or feeling uninspired. But with AI tools, you get a simple solution to this common problem: you can generate new and innovative ideas for your content using your audience's interests and preferences.

A recent study by eMarketer revealed that 58% of marketers using generative AI for content creation saw a big boost in performance. JPMorgan Chase used Persado's Gen AI to create ad copy and achieved a remarkable 450% increase in click-through rates (CTR) for their marketing campaigns. This shows just how impactful AI is in content creation and enhancing campaign performance in the marketing world.

Content creation plays a versatile and multifaceted role across various aspects of business operations. It is not limited to a single function but rather serves multiple purposes and can be applied in different contexts to achieve various goals. Creating engaging content and effective marketing strategies are important for businesses to connect with their audiences.

As we go into the nitty-gritty details of this chapter, we will uncover how ChatGPT is changing content creation and marketing, allowing businesses to create more engaging and impactful content that resonates with their audience on a deeper level. We will also explore the potential of ChatGPT in content writing with practical strategies and actionable tips to help you navigate the digital marketing field.

Revolution in Content Creation with ChatGPT

The business world thrives on efficient communication, and content plays a central role in achieving that. The approach to content creation is undergoing a metamorphosis with ChatGPT, offering a multitude of benefits that can significantly impact a business's reach and engagement. However, let's look at the numerous benefits ChatGPT provides businesses with:

Enhancing Efficiency

ChatGPT is like a tireless assistant who can handle multiple tasks. It helps tackle repetitive work like generating first drafts, social media captions, and even basic blog posts. This allows time for your writers and marketing teams to focus on strategy, in-depth research, and audience analysis. ChatGPT also helps brainstorm topics, suggest outlines, and even generate different creative angles to keep content fresh and engaging. This means that you can produce more content at a faster rate to maintain a consistent content pipeline and capitalize on marketing opportunities.

Automated Research and Data Analysis

With ChatGPT, you no longer have to spend hours sifting through mountains of information. ChatGPT can summarize key points, analyze data, identify trends, and even generate reports using specific prompts. This helps businesses create data-driven content that resonates with their target audience. It can also research and compile this information, ensuring the content is factually accurate and reflects current market trends to help your business tailor its content for maximum impact.

Streamlining Content Production Processes

ChatGPT acts as a catalyst, streamlining workflows and breaking down content creation into manageable steps. If you are experiencing writer's block, ChatGPT can spark inspiration, helping you overcome creative roadblocks. If you need to adapt content for different platforms or audiences, ChatGPT can rewrite existing content in new formats or tones, saving you time and resources. This streamlined approach promotes consistency and quality control across all content channels, ensuring a cohesive brand message is delivered to various audiences.

Tailored Content for Specific Audiences

ChatGPT analyzes user data and preferences, allowing businesses to personalize content for different demographics or customer segments. It can help craft marketing materials that speak directly to a specific audience's needs and interests. ChatGPT can achieve this level of personalization by suggesting language, examples, and even content formats that resonate with your target audience. This approach leads to higher engagement and better conversion rates.

Optimizing Content for Search Engine Visibility

Keywords are the gateway to search engine visibility. ChatGPT understands search engine algorithms and can suggest optimal content structures to improve discoverability. This might include crafting clear and concise headlines, organizing the content with headings and subheadings, and suggesting internal linking to connect related content on your website. These seemingly small tweaks recommended by ChatGPT can have a significant impact on search engine ranking and organic website traffic.

Prompts for Enhancing Content Creation

Here's a series of thirty ChatGPT prompt examples tailored for generating different types of content:

- **Blog Post Introduction**: Write an engaging introduction for a blog post about the benefits of using AI in content creation.
- **Product Description**: Craft a compelling product description for our latest smartwatch model, focusing on its key features, such as heart rate monitoring, GPS tracking, and waterproof design, and highlighting the benefits of convenience, health tracking, and style.
- **Social Media Post**: Craft a catchy social media post promoting a new line of skincare products, highlighting their natural ingredients and eco-friendly packaging.
- **Email Newsletter:** Draft a friendly and informative email newsletter announcing a special sale event to loyal customers.
- **How-To Guide**: Write a step-by-step guide on how to create a budget for beginners.
- **Listicle**: Create a listicle featuring the top ten travel destinations for adventure seekers.
- **Product Review**: Write a detailed review of *The Alchemist* by Paulo Coelho, highlighting its plot, characters, and themes. Include your reflections on the book's impact and relevance to society.
- **FAQ Page**: Create an FAQ page for a software company, addressing common questions about their products.
- **Recipe**: Share a delicious and easy-to-make recipe for homemade chocolate chip cookies.
- **Company Announcement**: Draft a company announcement introducing a new CEO and outlining their vision for the future.

- **Press Release**: Write a press release announcing a partnership between two tech companies.
- **Job Description**: Craft a compelling job description for a marketing manager position at a startup.
- **About Us Page**: Create an engaging "About Us" page for a fashion brand, highlighting its history and values.
- **Ebook Introduction**: Write an intriguing introduction for an ebook about the future of remote work.
- **White Paper**: Write a white paper on the role of AI in improving patient outcomes in oncology treatment.
- **Travel Guide:** Craft a detailed travel guide for a weekend getaway to Paris, France, highlighting the best attractions, restaurants, and activities for a memorable experience.
- **Event Invitation**: Craft an elegant event invitation for a charity gala, including event details and RSVP instructions.
- **Customer Testimonial**: Write a customer testimonial for a fitness app, highlighting its effectiveness and user-friendliness.
- **Website Homepage Copy**: Develop compelling copy for the homepage of a sustainable fashion brand, showcasing its commitment to eco-friendly practices.
- **Advertisement Copy**: Write a catchy advertisement for a new energy drink, highlighting its refreshing taste and energy-boosting properties.
- **Podcast Episode Description**: Create a captivating episode description for a podcast episode featuring an interview with a renowned author.

- **Video Script**: Write a script for a promotional video showcasing the features of a new smartphone.
- **Survey Questions**: Develop survey questions to gather feedback from customers about their shopping experience.
- **Infographic Outline**: Design an infographic outline explaining the impact of regular exercise on mental and physical health, including benefits such as improved mood, increased energy levels, better sleep, and a reduced risk of chronic diseases.
- **Presentation Slides**: Design an outline for engaging presentation slides on a pitch deck to secure funding for a healthcare startup focused on developing AI-powered diagnostic tools for early cancer detection.
- **Course Syllabus**: Develop a course syllabus for a beginner's photography course, outlining topics and learning objectives.
- **Email Template**: Create a customizable email template for sending out monthly newsletters.
- **Product Comparison Chart**: Design a product comparison chart comparing the features and prices of different smartphones.

Prompts for Marketing Content Creation

Here are some ChatGPT prompts you should look to try in your free time on marketing content creation:

- **Writing Blog Headlines**: Write a compelling headline for a blog post about (insert topic).

- **Creating Meta Descriptions for Blogs**: Write a meta description for our (insert blog title, keyword, or topic) blog that will maximize click-through rates.
- **Compiling Ideas for How-To Guides**: Compile a list of ideas for a series of informative how-to guides or tutorials on (insert topic).
- **Generating Newsletter Subject Line Options**: Create engaging subject line options for an upcoming newsletter that will highlight (insert topic or theme).
- **Compiling Ideas for Gated Content**: Compile a list of ten ideas for gated content, such as downloadable templates or an ebook for a company in (insert industry).
- **Providing a List of SEO-Optimized Keywords**: Provide a list of fifteen keywords for blog posts to optimize our website's SEO performance (insert additional information for context).
- **Turning Your Content Strategy into a Pitch to Stakeholders**: Summarize our proposed content strategy so we can pitch its benefits to stakeholders and upper management. (Ensure to provide ChatGPT with a detailed description of your content strategy, which may include your objectives, target audience, content themes, and any other relevant details.)
- **Email Marketing**: Creating email greetings: Craft a personalized email greeting for a campaign promoting our new line of sustainable activewear to environmentally conscious fitness enthusiasts.
- **Drafting CTAs**: Draft options for a persuasive CTA on

our landing page to promote our upcoming webinar on (topic).

- **Increasing Click-Through Rates**: Suggest innovative ways to increase click-through rates for our weekly newsletter.
- **Creating Customer Feedback Surveys**: Create a copy for a customer feedback survey email to be sent after a customer service interaction.
- **Proposing A/B Testing Headlines**: Propose two different email headlines that we can use for A/B testing in our next promotional campaign for our line of organic skincare products targeting Gen-Zs and millennials.
- **Composing Re-engagement Emails**: Compose a re-engagement email intended for customers who haven't made a purchase in the last six months.
- **Generating Campaign Ideas**: Generate ideas for a summer-themed email marketing campaign to promote our seasonal products.
- **Providing Email Templates**: Provide a framework or template that we can use for all of our marketing campaign emails.
- **Creating Taglines**: Create a memorable tagline or slogan for our brand, focusing on our commitment to sustainability.
- **Creating Copy for Instagram Stories**: Craft a series of Instagram Stories featuring tips and tricks on how to use a skincare product.
- **Writing Brand Guidelines:** Write a set of guidelines to

ensure brand consistency across all marketing materials, focusing on our brand voice and tone.

- **Create an Informative Video Script That Demonstrates How Your Product** (let's say, a smart home security system) **Solves a Common Problem** (prevents break-ins and provides peace of mind for homeowners).

Integrating AI into Overall Marketing Strategy

Integrating AI into content marketing can significantly enhance your overall marketing strategy. Here's how you can strategically leverage AI:

Define Your Goals and Target Audience

- **Start with a Clear Understanding of Your Marketing Objectives:** What do you want to achieve? Increase brand awareness? Drive sales? Generate leads? Knowing your objectives will guide your AI selection.
- **Identify Your Target Audience:** Analyze your target audience's demographics, interests, and online behavior. Who are you trying to reach with your marketing efforts? Understanding their demographics, interests, and online behavior is crucial for successful AI implementation. This will help inform you on how you can leverage AI for personalized marketing efforts.

Identify Areas Where AI Can Add Value

- **Content Creation:** Explore AI tools for brainstorming ideas, generating content outlines, or even writing initial drafts.
- **Personalization:** Use AI to tailor your marketing messages, email campaigns, recommendations, social media ads, and offers based on user data and behavior.
- **Customer Journey Optimization:** AI-powered chatbots can answer customer inquiries 24/7, improving the customer experience at various touchpoints. It can analyze customer interactions and help suggest improvements to your marketing funnel for a smoother customer experience.
- **Marketing Analytics and Optimization:** AI can analyze vast amounts of marketing data to identify trends, optimize campaign performance, and predict customer behavior. This allows for data-driven marketing decisions and improved ROI.

Choose the Right AI Tools

- **Research and Compare:** With a plethora of AI marketing tools available, research and compare their features and functionalities. Look for tools that address your specific needs and integrate seamlessly with your existing marketing stack.
- **Start Small and Scale Up:** Don't try to overhaul your entire marketing strategy overnight. Begin by integrating AI into a single aspect of your marketing,

like content creation or email personalization. As you gain experience, you can expand your use of AI tools.

Prioritize Data Management

- **Clean and Organized Data:** AI relies on high-quality data to function effectively. Ensure your customer data is clean, organized, and up-to-date.
- **Data Security and Privacy:** Comply with data privacy regulations like the General Data Protection Regulation (GDPR) or the California Consumer Privacy Act (CCPA). Be transparent with customers about how you collect and use their data for AI-powered marketing initiatives.

Monitor and Measure Results

- **Track Performance Metrics:** Closely monitor the performance of your AI-powered marketing campaigns. Track key metrics like conversion rates, click-through rates, and customer engagement to assess the impact of AI on your marketing strategy.
- **Refine and Adapt:** Based on your results, continuously refine your AI integration strategy. Be prepared to adapt your approach as AI technologies evolve and customer behavior changes.

Wrap-Up

In summary, the integration of AI into content marketing offers numerous benefits, from improving content planning and SEO optimization to providing valuable information about marketing campaigns. However, the data-driven capabilities of AI extend far beyond content creation and marketing. AI plays a crucial role in strategic business decision-making by processing big chunks of data, which can be beneficial in understanding current and recasting future trends.

In the next chapter, we will look deeper into AI's role in data analysis and collection, exploring how businesses can leverage AI to gain competitive advantage. We will discuss various AI-powered techniques and tools for data analysis, including predictive analytics, sentiment analysis, and customer segmentation.

6. Data-Driven Decisions

The ability to make informed decisions on time and accurately can mean the difference between success and failure. Businesses deal with data every day, ranging from customer feedback to operational metrics, which can be overwhelming to analyze and interpret manually. This is where artificial intelligence (AI) comes in to help your business collect, process, and use data for better decision-making.

A study by Deloitte found that implementing artificial intelligence within a mining business allowed for improved data processes, making them eighteen times faster than what was previously done in the field. This remarkable leap explains the potential of AI in diverse industries by using data that was previously inaccessible or time-consuming to obtain to make accurate business decisions.

This chapter will explore the use of AI in facilitating the collection and analysis of data. We will look into real-world examples and case studies to explain how to use AI to make informed, data-driven decisions that drive success and create growth opportunities.

What Is Data Analysis?

Data analysis is the process of examining, cleaning, transforming, and interpreting data to extract useful information, inform conclusions, and support decision-making. It involves various techniques and methods to reveal patterns, trends, relationships, and insights from datasets. This helps you gain a deeper understanding of business operations, customers, and market dynamics.

In essence, data analysis is like mining for gold within a big mine of information. Just as miners sift through rocks and debris to find precious nuggets of gold, data analysts sift through vast amounts of data to discover information that will boost business growth.

One of the key aspects of data analysis is the use of statistical techniques and algorithms to identify patterns and relationships within the data. For example, in retail, data analysts may use sales data to check for correlations between certain products, customer demographics, and purchasing behaviors. Analyzing these patterns helps retailers optimize their product offerings, pricing strategies, and marketing campaigns to better meet customer needs and preferences.

Data analysis often uses visualization tools and techniques to present findings clearly and understandably. Visualizations, such as charts, graphs, and dashboards, help you better understand complex data patterns for decision-making. A hospital may use interactive dashboards to visualize patient data so that healthcare professionals can observe trends in patient health and make informed treatment decisions.

Real-life examples of data analysis cut across various industries. For instance, in finance, banks use data analysis to detect fraudulent transactions and assess credit risk. In manufacturing, companies use predictive maintenance techniques to analyze equipment sensor data and prevent costly downtime. In e-commerce, retailers use data analysis to personalize product recommendations and improve the shopping experience for customers.

Why Is Data Analysis Important?

Data analysis is important for businesses to make informed decisions and gain a competitive edge. Let's explore these aspects with examples:

Informed Decision-Making

Data analysis helps you make decisions based on evidence rather than intuition or guesswork. Access to accurate and relevant information is important for making informed decisions in business. AI tools like ChatGPT can process large amounts of data accurately to provide insights that humans might miss. This can help your business understand market trends, customer preferences, and potential risks, allowing them to make strategic decisions that lead to growth and success. For instance, Hulu uses data analysis to recommend movies and TV shows to its users. This works by analyzing viewing patterns and preferences and, hence, suggesting content that aligns with individual tastes for higher user satisfaction and retention.

Improved Understanding

Data analysis allows businesses to gain deeper knowledge of various aspects of their operations, customers, and market trends. Analyzing data from various sources with AI can help identify trends that provide useful insights. This deep understanding allows you to maximize opportunities and adapt strategies accordingly. For instance, Amazon uses data analysis tools to optimize its supply chain management on inventory levels, shipping times, and customer demand to ensure timely deliveries.

Competitive Advantage

Analyzing data provides you with a competitive edge in information that others may overlook. Information can be a source of differentiation in the marketplace. Companies that use data analytics can tailor their products or services more precisely to meet customer needs, setting themselves apart from competitors. For example, Walmart uses data analysis to optimize its pricing strategy. They can adjust prices in real time to remain competitive and maximize profits by analyzing sales data and market trends.

Risk Management

Data analysis plays a significant role in identifying and mitigating risks for businesses. Businesses can identify potential risks early on to allow them to take proactive measures to minimize or eliminate these risks. In the insurance industry, data analysis is used to assess risk factors such as age, health, and driving record to determine insurance premiums. This can help insurance companies accurately assess the level of risk associated with each policyholder and adjust premiums according to the data results.

Efficient Resource Allocation

Effective resource allocation is essential for optimizing operational efficiency and maximizing ROI. Data analysis helps businesses identify areas where resources can be allocated more efficiently. For instance, retailers analyze sales data to identify high-demand products and allocate inventory as required. Using predictive analytics models can help retailers forecast demand trends and adjust inventory levels to meet customer demands, thereby minimizing stockouts and excess inventory.

Continuous Improvement

Analyzing data facilitates continuous improvement by providing insights into performance metrics and areas for enhancement. Analyzing key performance indicators (KPIs) and feedback data can help discover areas of weakness and implement strategies for improvement. Manufacturing companies analyze production data to identify bottlenecks and optimize manufacturing processes. Using statistical process control techniques, such as Six Sigma, can identify sources of variation and implement corrective actions to improve product quality and reduce defects.

New Business Opportunities

Data-driven decisions help businesses spot and capitalize on new business opportunities. Data analyzed from various sources, such as market research, customer feedback, and competitor analysis, can help recognize untapped markets and niche segments. Analyzing website traffic data may reveal a growing interest in a particular product category, prompting businesses to expand their offerings in that area. Data-driven decisions also help businesses make strategic investments and partnerships that align with market trends and customer preferences.

Data Analysis Process

The data analysis process typically consists of several key stages, each of which is important for deriving meaningful insights from data. Here's an overview of the process:

- **Data Collection:** Data collection is the process of gathering relevant data from various sources, such as databases, surveys, spreadsheets, APIs, sensors, text documents, or external datasets. This step involves identifying the data needed for analysis, obtaining permission to access the data, and ensuring that the data is accurate and comprehensive.

- **Data Cleaning:** Data cleaning, also known as data preprocessing, is the process of identifying and correcting errors, inconsistencies, or missing values in the dataset. This step involves tasks such as removing duplicates, filling in missing values, correcting typos or formatting errors, and standardizing data formats. This is to ensure that the dataset is accurate, reliable, and suitable for analysis.

- **Exploratory Data Analysis (EDA):** EDA involves visually and statistically exploring the dataset to gain information and spot patterns or relationships between variables. This includes generating summary statistics, creating data visualizations (such as histograms, scatter plots, or heatmaps), and performing statistical tests or calculations. EDA helps analysts understand the structure of the data, detect outliers or anomalies, and generate hypotheses for further analysis.

- **Data Transformation:** Once the data is cleaned, it may need to be transformed into a format suitable for analysis. This could involve aggregating data, creating new variables, or applying mathematical transformations to normalize the data distribution. For example, converting text data into numerical values or normalizing data to a standard scale.

- **Model Building:** After the data is transformed, statistical or machine learning models are used to analyze the data and extract insights. This could involve regression analysis, clustering, classification, or other modeling techniques, depending on the nature of the data and the analysis goals.

- **Interpretation and Visualization:** Once the model is built and analyzed, the final step is to interpret the results and visualize them in a way that is easy to understand. This may involve creating charts, graphs, or other visualizations to represent the data and highlight key findings. The goal is to communicate the results gained from the data analysis process in a clear and meaningful way so that informed decisions can be made based on the findings.

- **Deployment:** Finally, the results derived from the analysis need to be deployed into actionable strategies or solutions. This may involve implementing recommendations, updating business processes, or integrating analytical tools into decision-making workflows. Continuous monitoring and refinement are crucial to ensuring the ongoing effectiveness of the data analysis process.

Utilizing ChatGPT in Data Analysis

Data analysis is a complex process that often requires expertise in programming and statistical methods. With ChatGPT's Advanced Data Analysis feature, data analysis becomes more accessible and efficient, even for users without extensive programming knowledge. This feature, available exclusively to premium (paid) accounts, uses the capabilities of GPT-4 to streamline the data analysis process and enhance the accuracy of results.

ChatGPT's Advanced Data Analysis feature is a tool integrated into the GPT-4 model to facilitate data analysis tasks by allowing users to upload data directly to ChatGPT for analysis. This feature is particularly useful for users seeking to explore data, write and test code, and solve data-related problems with the help of AI tools. Users can significantly increase the efficiency and accuracy of their data analysis workflows by running code directly on ChatGPT.

Key Features and Benefits

- **Direct Data Upload:** You can upload your data directly to ChatGPT, eliminating the need for external software or platforms. This integration streamlines the data analysis process and reduces friction in accessing and analyzing datasets.
- **Code Execution:** With ChatGPT's Advanced Data Analysis feature, users can write and execute code within the ChatGPT interface. This functionality allows you to perform a wide range of data manipulation, transformation, and analysis tasks without leaving the platform.
- **Increased Use Cases:** The Advanced Data Analysis feature expands the use cases for the model across various domains and industries by enabling code execution directly within ChatGPT. Whether you are analyzing financial data, conducting market research, or performing scientific experiments, ChatGPT's AI capabilities can assist in the analysis process.

- **Enhanced Accuracy:** The integration of data analysis capabilities into ChatGPT ensures a higher level of accuracy in the output produced by the model. Using GPT-4's advanced language understanding and reasoning abilities helps you trust the results generated by ChatGPT for your data analysis tasks.

How It Works

To use ChatGPT's Advanced Data Analysis feature, you simply need to upload your dataset and write the necessary code within the ChatGPT interface. ChatGPT then processes the code and executes it on the uploaded data, providing users with insights, visualizations, and analysis results. This workflow enables you to run through your data easily, refine their analysis, and make informed decisions based on the data.

Advantages of AI-Driven Analysis

AI-driven data analysis offers several advantages that can significantly improve the efficiency and effectiveness of data processing and interpretation.

- **Speed:** AI algorithms can process large volumes of data in a fraction of the time it would take a human analyst. This helps businesses make faster decisions and respond to changes. This speed is valuable in industries where real-time information is important, such as finance, healthcare, and e-commerce.

- **Scalability:** Since AI-powered data analysis tools are highly scalable, they are capable of handling large datasets with ease. As businesses generate increasingly large volumes of data, AI provides the scalability needed to analyze and handle the increased workload without a proportional increase in resources.
- **Predictive Analytics:** AI is capable of generating predictive models that forecast future trends, behaviors, and outcomes based on historical data. Businesses can anticipate customer needs, identify potential risks, and make proactive decisions with the help of predictive analytics.

ChatGPT Prompts for Data Analysis

Here are some ChatGPT prompts you can use to analyze data:

- Generate a summary of the key trends in the dataset provided.
- Provide insights into customer behavior based on the given dataset.
- Analyze the correlation between two specific variables in the dataset.
- Create visualizations (charts, graphs) to illustrate the patterns in the data.
- Identify outliers in the dataset and explain their potential impact on the analysis.
- Compare the performance of different product lines based on the sales data.
- Predict future trends based on historical data provided.

- Segment the customer base into distinct groups based on their purchasing behavior using the data provided.
- Evaluate the effectiveness of a marketing campaign using the available data.
- Recommend personalized product offerings based on customer preferences.
- Identify factors that influence customer satisfaction using survey data.
- Analyze the impact of pricing changes on sales volume.
- Predict customer churn based on historical customer data.
- Determine the optimal pricing strategy for a new product based on market research data.
- Analyze website traffic data to identify opportunities for improving user experience.
- Evaluate the performance of different advertising channels based on conversion rates.
- Identify trends in social media engagement that can inform content strategy.
- Analyze product reviews to identify common themes and sentiments.
- Forecast demand for a product based on historical sales data.
- Provide recommendations for inventory management based on sales forecasting data.

Wrap-Up

As we conclude our exploration of AI-driven data analysis, it is important to recognize the broader implications of these capabilities. The use of AI in data-driven decision-making extends far beyond improving operational efficiencies; it has the potential to increase sales and lead generation strategies. Leveraging AI analysis can help businesses directly improve their sales strategies and lead generation. As we move forward, we will look at how AI technologies can boost sales and increase success in your business.

7. Sales and Lead Generation

Sales are the stronghold of many businesses, and entrepreneurs are looking for better and new ways to drive sales and increase profits. According to Ringover Statistics, businesses could save an estimated $89.07 billion per year if salespeople used AI to complete data entry and non-sales-related tasks, which currently take up 70% of their time. Moreover, integrating AI tools into the sales process has led to a 50% increase in sales leads for many companies. This means that businesses that use AI tools in their sales strategies and lead-generation processes stand to gain significant advantages in today's competitive marketplace.

In this chapter, we will explore in detail how AI and ChatGPT offer substantial advantages in sales strategies and lead generation processes. These tools have the potential to transform sales operations and increase profit, from automating routine tasks to enhancing customer interactions. We will show you how to leverage AI tools to identify and connect with highly qualified prospects.

Using ChatGPT in Sales

ChatGPT in sales processes marks a significant change in how businesses engage with customers and drive revenue. Gone are the days of cold calls and generic pitches. Today, savvy sales-people use AI tools to gain a competitive edge. ChatGPT isn't just about efficiency; although it excels at automating tedious tasks, it is also about using AI insights to make smarter decisions, develop winning strategies, and close more deals.

With ChatGPT, you can tap into a wealth of information to magnify sales success, from personalized customer interactions to predictive analytics. This tool can help your sales teams in various ways to improve efficiency and effectiveness and ulti-mately sell more. Here are some key use cases:

Sales Forecasting

AI algorithms can predict sales by ingesting data from your CRM (customer relationship management) system, marketing automation platform, and even social media interactions. They then analyze factors like sales stage, customer demo-graphics, past buying behavior, and economic indicators. Based on this analysis, the AI generates a forecast that predicts the likelihood of closing each deal in your pipeline. Your sales team can focus their energy on the most promising opportu-nities by prioritizing leads based on their predicted closing probability, leading to a more efficient allocation of resources and time.

Summarize and Provide Action Items

Sales calls and meetings are crucial for building relationships and understanding customer needs. However, capturing key takeaways and outlining the next steps can be time-consuming. AI steps in as your virtual assistant, summarizing these interactions and providing clear action items. You can integrate AI-powered tools with your calendar and recording software.

After each call or meeting, the AI analyzes the recorded audio or video, extracting key points, decisions made, and next steps. This information is then presented in a concise and easily digestible format, often within your CRM system. With clear action items readily available, you are held accountable for moving the sales process forward. This promotes a sense of urgency and ensures tasks don't slip through the cracks.

Analyze Sales Calls

Every sales call holds valuable insights, but sometimes, these insights can be buried beneath layers of conversation. AI-powered sales call analysis tools help you unearth these hidden gems, highlighting strengths and weaknesses in your sales conversations. Similar to call summarization, these tools analyze recordings, focusing on factors like word choice, tonality, and objection handling. The AI then provides insights into how well salespeople are communicating value propositions, handling objections, and building rapport. By identifying areas for improvement, you can develop more effective communication strategies for a more persuasive and engaging sales pitch.

Recommending Next Actions for Sales Reps

AI tools like Algolia and Userbot.ai can act as coaches, whispering sales strategies in your ear. With AI-powered recommendation tools, you analyze large amounts of data, and, based on this analysis, they can recommend the most effective next steps after every customer touchpoint. AI considers the specific context of each interaction. Did the customer express concerns about the price? The AI might suggest offering a discount or financing option. Did they mention a specific product feature? The AI could recommend tailoring the pitch to highlight that feature's benefits. This ensures you are putting your efforts where they will yield the highest return and increase your efficiency.

Generating Sales Emails and Subject Lines That Convert

Crafting compelling email copy can be time-consuming, and, let's be honest, sometimes inspiration runs dry. But AI can step in and become your email writing partner. It can help you write compelling subject lines. Subject lines are the first impression—they determine whether your email gets opened or relegated to the trash.

AI can analyze proven subject line structures and high-performing email campaigns to generate attention-grabbing subject lines that entice customers to click. It can also personalize email content beyond simply inserting a name and suggesting email copy that speaks directly to the customer's needs and interests. This personalization can significantly increase open rates and engagement.

Identifying New In-Market Leads

Prospecting—finding new potential customers—is a fundamental aspect of sales. However, traditional methods can be time-consuming and yield mixed results. AI tools like Salesloft, HubSpot, Outreach.oi, etc., can help you with lead generation by monitoring social media conversations and spotting potential customers who are expressing needs or frustrations that your product or service can address. These tools constantly scan social media platforms like a hawk, looking for conversations relevant to your business and picking out keywords and phrases related to your industry, products, or services, especially those that signal a problem or need.

It then analyzes the tone of a post, recognizing frustration or a desire for solutions—prime lead territory and identifies specific users who might be interested in your offerings based on keywords, brand, or product category mentions. AI assigns "scores" to potential leads based on their engagement and fits with your ideal customer profile, helping your sales team prioritize their efforts. With AI predictive modeling abilities, it can use historical sales data and customer behavior to predict which leads are most likely to convert, with the highest potential for closing a deal.

Predicting Likelihood to Close

AI-powered sales tools like Salesforce Einstein, Clari, Drift, etc., can help predict the probability of a prospect becoming a customer by analyzing historical sales data and buyer interactions. AI tools use information from various sources, including customer demographics, past interactions (emails, calls, website visits), and industry trends, then search for patterns and correlations between past customer behavior and successful deals.

These patterns might include specific buying signals, response times to emails, or website pages visited. Based on the discovered patterns, a model that assigns a "score" to each lead is created, indicating the likelihood of closing the deal. This score is a powerful tool for prioritizing your efforts and resources and identifying leads with the highest closing probability. This ensures you are spending more time nurturing the most promising opportunities.

Predicting Readiness to Buy

Timing is everything in sales. Reaching out to a prospect who isn't ready to buy can backfire. AI can help you predict a prospect's readiness to buy, ensuring your approach is well-timed and impactful. It works by analyzing a prospect's online behavior, social media activity, and interactions with your brand to identify buying signals.

These signals might include downloading white papers, attending webinars, or visiting specific product pages on your website. When AI detects a prospect nearing their buying window, it can trigger automated outreach or send you an alert to initiate a conversation. Reaching out at the right time when a prospect is actively considering a purchase can significantly increase your chances of closing the deal.

Automatic Lead Scoring

AI-powered lead scoring helps you reduce time spent chasing unqualified leads. AI algorithms use the data of your existing customers and past sales to check for patterns and characteristics that are common among successful conversions. Once these patterns are established, the AI assigns a score to each new lead.

This score reflects the likelihood that the lead will convert into a sale. Leads with high scores are likely your ideal customers, the ones who are most interested in your product or service. With leads ranked by their conversion potential, you can use fewer resources and waste less time on clients. Low-scoring leads aren't ignored; they can be nurtured with targeted campaigns or passed on to a different sales team.

AI-Powered Competitive Intelligence

Staying ahead of the competition is important in sales. However, manually monitoring competitor activity can be a daunting task. AI tools like Kompyte, G2Crowd, Craft, Wappalyzer, etc., can offer you real-time information about what your competitors are up to. AI tools can crawl the web, social media platforms, and industry publications to gather information about your competitors. They analyze news articles, press releases, product launches, and marketing campaigns, building a comprehensive picture of your competitor's activities.

This information is then processed by AI algorithms to reveal a competitor's focus on a specific product line, a new marketing campaign they have launched, or even changes in their pricing structure. This helps you to make informed decisions, identify areas where your product or service excels compared to the competition, develop targeted marketing campaigns to counter their strategies and adjust your pricing strategy to remain competitive.

Leveraging ChatGPT for Lead Generation

Generating leads is the lifeblood of any business. Using ChatGPT for lead generation offers a unique approach to nurturing potential customers. It helps you engage with leads conversationally, providing personalized interactions that fit individual needs and preferences. However, let's look at how ChatGPT can play a role in each stage of lead generation.

Website Chatbots

Gone are the days of limited-hour lead capture. ChatGPT chatbots can act as virtual salespersons, engaging website visitors in conversations, qualifying leads, and scheduling appointments—even while you sleep. ChatGPT Zapier allows you to create chatbots that can hold natural conversations, understand visitor intent, and respond with relevant information. With ChatGPT chatbots integrated into your website, you will never miss a potential lead again. It can answer questions and capture leads even outside of business hours, keeping your lead generation engine running around the clock.

Social Media Management

Social media is a gold mine for leads, but managing multiple platforms and creating engaging content can be overwhelming. If you are struggling with writer's block, ChatGPT can help you generate engaging social media posts, captions, and even scripts for video content. When you identify relevant conversations and potential leads on social media platforms, you can paste them on ChatGPT to craft personalized messages to initiate conversations and nurture leads further down the funnel. It also makes responding to social media comments and messages easier by assisting you in handling basic inquiries and promoting positive interactions with potential customers.

Email Campaigns

Crafting personalized email campaigns that resonate with your audience is very important for lead nurturing. ChatGPT can streamline your email marketing efforts by creating attention-grabbing subject lines and tailoring email content to specific segments of your audience, increasing open rates and engagement. If you are unsure of which email format or call to action works best, ChatGPT can help you generate variations and run A/B tests to optimize your email campaigns for maximum lead conversion.

Content Creation

High-quality content is a magnet for leads. However, consistently generating informative and engaging content can be a challenge. ChatGPT can help in generating informative blog posts and articles on topics relevant to your target audience. It can assist you with research, outlining, and even writing engaging content that positions you as an industry thought leader. Aside from website content and blog posts, it can aid in developing valuable lead magnets like ebooks and white papers to capture leads in exchange for their contact information.

Cold Outreach

Cold outreach, the art of contacting potential customers who haven't expressed initial interest, is often a numbers game. ChatGPT can transform this process from a monotonous chore into an easier process. To do this, you need to provide

ChatGPT with basic information about your ideal customer profile and target audience.

It can then generate personalized email templates or social media messages that resonate with their specific needs and pain points rather than generic pitches. It can also personalize greetings, insert relevant company details, and even tailor the tone of the message based on the recipient's demographics or online behavior. This level of personalization can significantly increase response rates and engagement.

Lead Qualification

Qualifying leads and identifying those with a genuine interest in your product or service is a critical aspect of your business. ChatGPT can help you develop a scoring system based on predefined criteria like industry, company size, and website behavior. ChatGPT makes chatbots feel more human, encouraging leads to share details. It can ask qualifying questions to identify promising leads based on their needs while tailoring responses and content based on the lead's interests, keeping them engaged. This allows you to focus your sales team's efforts on qualified leads most likely to convert.

CRM Integration

A well-maintained CRM (customer relationship management) system is vital for tracking leads and nurturing them through the sales funnel. ChatGPT can bridge the gap between your lead generation efforts and your CRM. Leads interact with a

ChatGPT-powered chatbot, sharing details and answers while key information like contact details, conversation history, and lead qualification responses are sent to your CRM. This saves time and minimizes the risk of errors. Based on the information in your CRM, ChatGPT can help you create targeted email sequences or social media campaigns tailored to each lead's specific needs and interests. This ensures your communication resonates with each lead and keeps them engaged throughout the sales cycle.

Prompts for Lead Generation

Here are a few ChatGPT prompts you can copy and paste into its chatbots for lead generation:

- Generate a list of potential leads for our new product launch in the healthcare industry.
- Craft an email template to engage potential leads and encourage them to sign up for a webinar.
- Create a social media post to promote our latest ebook and capture leads.
- Develop a lead magnet idea that will attract potential leads interested in our services.
- Write a blog post that addresses the common pain points of our target audience and includes a call-to-action to capture leads.
- Brainstorm creative ways to use interactive content, such as quizzes or assessments, to capture leads.
- Draft a series of follow-up emails to nurture leads who have shown interest but have not yet converted.

- Create a landing page that highlights the benefits of our product or service and encourages visitors to provide their contact information.
- Design a lead capture form for our website that is simple, user-friendly, and optimized for conversions.
- Develop a content calendar that includes lead generation-focused content to attract and engage potential leads.
- Write a script for a cold outreach campaign to reach out to potential leads via email or LinkedIn.
- Create a lead scoring system to prioritize and qualify leads based on their level of engagement and interest.
- Optimize our website's SEO in the article provided to attract organic traffic and generate more leads.
- Design a social media advertising campaign targeting our ideal customer profile to generate leads.
- Create a webinar or virtual event that provides valuable information to our target audience and captures leads.
- Develop a referral program to incentivize existing customers to refer new leads to us.
- Write a case study showcasing how our product or service has helped a client, with a call-to-action to contact us for more information.
- Craft a series of lead nurturing emails to guide leads through the sales funnel and convert them into customers.
- Create a lead magnet that offers a free trial or demo of our product to capture leads' contact information.
- Develop a strategy to engage with leads on social media and build relationships that lead to conversions.

Wrap-Up

As we have explored the impact of AI on sales and lead generation, it's clear that these technologies are important in our day-
to-day business activities. The information gained from effective sales and lead generation strategies can directly inform
product development and design, creating a feedback loop that
positively impacts business growth. Next, we will discuss how
businesses can use AI tools to streamline the design process and
create products that resonate with their target audience.

8. Product Development and Design

The success of a product relies not only on its functionality but also on its ability to relate to users and meet their needs. As businesses continue to grow and stay ahead of the competition, the role of artificial intelligence (AI) and ChatGPT in product development and design has become increasingly prominent.

According to Unbounce Statistics, more than 80% of businesses believe that AI tools will positively impact their business in three years or less. This explains the growing recognition among businesses of the potential of AI to improve designs and product development. Here, we will look at the role of AI and ChatGPT in product development and design, explaining how these technologies can ease the ideation process, enhance user-centric designs, and refine product functionality for market success.

AI's Role in Ideation and Conceptualization

The ideation stage of product development is often messy and unpredictable. Ideas come in fits and starts, leaving you struggling to find that "next big thing." But with AI, you can improve your ideation and conceptualization process, from sparking creative thinking to conducting market research. However, here's how AI can help in generating product ideas and conducting insightful market research:

Idea Generation

If you are feeling out of ideas, you can provide ChatGPT with a broad starting point related to your industry or target market. It can help you generate a list of random prompts or ideas to spark your creativity. What you need to do is feed ChatGPT data on current market trends, competitor analysis, and even social media conversations. It can then use this information to generate product ideas that directly address unmet needs and capitalize on emerging market opportunities. Don't let your initial ideas exist in a vacuum. Use ChatGPT to analyze your product concepts against market data, suggesting features that better align with customer preferences and buying habits.

Market Research

Don't just generate ideas; validate them with market research. ChatGPT's advanced data analysis can be used to analyze social media conversations and online reviews. It will help you understand customer pain points and desires, allowing you to tailor your product ideas to address market demands.

Also, if you are struggling to define your ideal customer profile, provide ChatGPT with demographic data and psychographic information to help you create detailed customer personas. This helps in generating product ideas that cater to their specific needs and preferences. Also, analyzing your competitor's market can help you understand the emotional triggers and values associated with your competitor's products to develop ideas that compete functionally.

Prototyping

While ChatGPT can't physically build prototypes, it can play a role in the pre-prototyping phase. Once you have a promising idea, ChatGPT can assist you in prototyping. You need to describe your idea to ChatGPT and let it generate basic sketches, wireframes, or even user interface mockups for quick testing of the functionality and user experience without extensive design resources.

It can also check for potential design flaws before any physical prototypes are built. When ChatGPT analyzes the technical aspects of your product concept, it might flag potential hurdles related to feasibility or integration with existing technologies. This foresight allows you to address these challenges early on to simplify the prototyping process.

Testing and Gathering Feedback

Before a full-fledged launch, testing and gathering user feedback are important. If you have multiple design variations for your product concept, ChatGPT can help you create A/B testing scenarios, presenting different versions and analyzing their preferences, which allows you to identify the most appealing features. You can also use ChatGPT to analyze market research data and generate detailed user personas.

These detailed profiles of your ideal customers can guide your user testing by ensuring you recruit participants who accurately represent your target audience. This allows you to develop a comprehensive set of user testing questions that target specific aspects of your product concept and user experience. This ensures you gather valuable data during the testing phase.

Marketing and Launch

The final stretch is bringing your product to market. As you prepare for launch, ChatGPT can assist in crafting a compelling marketing strategy. Don't settle for generic marketing messages; use ChatGPT's ability to understand user needs and generate persuasive language to create targeted marketing copy that resonates with your audience.

To do this, you need to provide it with your target audience demographics, online behavior, and product information to recognize the most effective marketing channels for reaching your ideal customers. It can also generate creative social media post ideas, captions, and even hashtags tailored to your target audience for maximum reach.

Why AI Is Important in Identifying Unmet Customer Needs

Understanding your customers' needs is paramount. However, traditional methods of customer feedback, like surveys and focus groups, can be limited. This is where AI steps in to help identify unmet customer needs you might have otherwise missed.

Customers don't always explicitly state their needs, especially negative ones. AI, particularly tools like sentiment analysis, can analyze customer data to pick out underlying frustrations and desires, even if they are not directly expressed. Traditional feedback methods often attract a specific demographic or those with strong opinions. AI can analyze data from a wider range of sources and reveal needs from diverse customer segments you might not have reached.

Social media platforms are a gold mine for customer sentiment. AI can help analyze the tone of social media posts and comments to sieve through positive and negative sentiments toward your brand, products, or services. Negative sentiment often highlights areas where customer needs are not being met.

Understanding your customers' needs allows you to develop products and services that directly address their pain points and desires, which eventually improve customer satisfaction and loyalty. Being at the forefront of customer needs allows you to differentiate yourself from competitors and capture a larger market share.

Enhancing Design with AI Insights

Before technology, design relied heavily on human creativity and intuition. While this approach has produced countless successful products and experiences, AI helps to enhance the design process. Let's look at how AI simulates and tests design concepts.

Step 1: Feeding the Machine

The first step involves equipping your AI tool with the necessary knowledge. This includes:

- **Design Concepts:** Provide high-fidelity mockups or detailed descriptions of the design concepts you plan to test.
- **Target Audience Data:** The more AI knows about your target user base, the better. Share demographics, online behavior patterns, and any relevant psychological insights about your audience.
- **Competitor Analysis:** Give AI a glimpse into the competitive landscape. Share information about existing products or similar designs to help it understand the context and identify potential differentiators for your concept.

Step 2: AI in Action

Once fed with this information, AI steps into action.

- **Simulating User Behavior:** AI tools can use advanced algorithms to create virtual users that interact with your design concepts. These simulations mimic real-world user behavior, allowing you to observe how users navigate the design, sort out areas of confusion, and assess overall usability.
- **Data-Driven Analysis:** AI doesn't just simulate; it analyzes. It tracks user interactions, clicks, time spent on specific elements, and even eye movements to spot patterns and areas of strength or weakness in your design.
- **A/B Testing on Steroids:** Imagine testing multiple variations of your design concept simultaneously. AI can facilitate A/B testing so you can compare different design elements and pick the version that performs best with your target audience.

Step 3: Human and Machine Synergy

As much as AI provides invaluable data and insights, it cannot replace human intuition. Here's how it happens:

- **Interpreting the Results:** AI-generated data requires human interpretation. Designers and marketing professionals will use their expertise to analyze the data and identify and make informed decisions about refining their design concepts based on AI's feedback.

- **Refining the Design:** With AI insights, you can choose concepts, address usability issues, optimize user experience, and create a design that fits with the target audience.

How to Use ChatGPT for Product Design

Using ChatGPT for product design can ease the design process and enhance creativity. Here's how you can use it for various aspects of product design:

Finding Feature-Specific Inspiration

ChatGPT can help generate ideas for specific features of your product. Describe the functionality or purpose you are looking for, and it will provide you with fresh, creative ideas. For example, if you are designing a new mobile app and need ideas for a unique onboarding process, you can describe the app's target audience, goals, and desired user experience to ChatGPT, and it will suggest new onboarding approaches.

Creating Feature Flow

A smooth feature flow is important for a positive user experience. ChatGPT can assist in designing the flow of features within your product. You can describe the user journey, interactions, and desired outcomes, and it will help map out the feature flow. For instance, if you are designing an e-commerce website and want to optimize the checkout process, you can describe the current flow and ask ChatGPT for suggestions on how to simplify and improve it.

Explaining Complex Terms

Great design often involves effectively communicating complex ideas to users. ChatGPT can simplify complex terms and concepts related to product design. If you are discussing technical details with stakeholders or team members who may not be familiar with design terminology, it can help you explain these concepts in plain language. For example, if you need to explain the concept of "user persona" to a non-designer, you can ask ChatGPT to provide a simple explanation that anyone can understand.

Understanding User Requirements

Understanding your target audience is the foundation of successful product design. ChatGPT can help designers understand user requirements by generating responses based on user input. By interacting with ChatGPT, you can gather insights into user preferences, frustrations, and expectations, which can inform the design process. For example, you can ask ChatGPT questions like, "What features would you like to see in a new smartphone?" or "How do you envision using this product in your daily life?" to gather user feedback.

Discovering Tools and Websites

The design world is a large ecosystem. ChatGPT can help you navigate it by discovering new tools and websites related to product design. You can ask ChatGPT for recommendations and help you find tools for prototyping, 3D modeling, graphic design, and other aspects of product design. Designers can ask ChatGPT, "Can you suggest any websites for finding inspiration for product design?" or "What tools do you recommend for creating interactive prototypes?"

Creating Better Prompts for AI Image Generators

AI image generators are becoming increasingly popular in the design process. Vague prompts lead to vague results. Use ChatGPT to refine your descriptions for AI image generators. It helps you create better prompts for AI image generators.

So, provide detailed information about color palettes, layouts, user interface elements, and overall design aesthetic to get the most out of your AI-generated visuals. Don't settle for the first version. Use the ChatGPT Plus subscription to analyze the AI-generated images and suggest refinements. Ask it to generate variations based on specific feedback, allowing you to explore different design directions and arrive at the optimal concept.

Create Design System Documentation

ChatGPT can assist in creating design system documentation, which includes guidelines, principles, and components used in a design project. You can ask ChatGPT to generate descriptions, explanations, or examples for design components, layouts, color schemes, typography, and more. If you are worried about inconsistencies creeping into your design system, ChatGPT can analyze your existing documentation and pick up any discrepancies to ensure your design language remains uniform across all projects.

Get Ideas for Design-Related Tasks

If you ever feel stuck, ChatGPT can be a valuable resource for generating ideas for design projects. By describing your project requirements or goals, you can suggest design concepts, layouts, color schemes, and visual styles. You can also use it to brainstorm creative solutions for specific design challenges or to explore new design directions.

Ask ChatGPT How It May Help You

Don't underestimate the power of a simple question. If you are unsure about the best approach for a specific design element, ask ChatGPT. It will provide insights and recommendations based on established design principles. It can also analyze your ideas and suggest potential solutions or any limitations to consider. Whether you are looking for design inspiration, advice on design tools and techniques, or tips on improving your design workflow, ChatGPT can offer great assistance.

Upskill

ChatGPT can be your design coach, helping you to expand your design skill set. Ask ChatGPT to explain specific design trends, software functionalities, or design principles that you don't understand. You can ask for learning resources, tutorials, or examples to improve your understanding of design concepts and practices. For example, you can ask for recommendations on books, courses, or workshops to expand your design expertise. This can help you stay updated with the latest developments in the field of design and enhance your design skills.

Prompts for Product Development

Here are some simple ChatGPT prompts you can use to guide your design process:

- Can you suggest innovative features for a fitness-tracking app aimed at improving user engagement?
- What are some design trends in e-commerce websites that can enhance the shopping experience?
- How can we improve the user interface of our mobile banking app to make it more intuitive for customers?
- Can you provide ideas for eco-friendly packaging designs for a new line of skincare products?
- What are some ways to incorporate gamification into a productivity app to motivate users?
- How can we redesign our website to increase conversion rates for our online store?

- Can you suggest improvements to the user onboarding process for a social networking app?
- What are some effective strategies for creating a cohesive brand identity across different products and platforms?
- How can we design a more user-friendly interface for our smart home device?
- What are the key elements to consider when designing a mobile game for a specific target audience?
- Can you provide examples of successful product launches and the strategies they used for market penetration?
- How can we use storytelling in our product packaging to create a stronger emotional connection with customers?
- What are some best practices for designing a mobile app that caters to users with accessibility needs?
- Can you suggest ways to incorporate user feedback into the iterative design process for a software application?
- What are some cost-effective materials and manufacturing methods for prototyping a new consumer electronics device?
- How can we optimize the user interface of our website for better performance on mobile devices?
- Can you provide examples of successful rebranding efforts and the impact they had on customer perception?
- What are some emerging technologies that could disrupt the market, and how can we prepare for them in our product development?

- How can we use data analytics to inform our product design decisions and improve user engagement?
- Can you suggest strategies for creating a seamless omnichannel experience for customers interacting with our brand across different platforms?

Wrap-Up

The role of AI and ChatGPT in product development and design cannot be overstated. These technologies can help streamline the ideation process and improve and enhance user-centric designs for market success. As businesses continue to use AI in their product development efforts, we can expect to see a wave of inventions that will reshape industries.

The efficiencies gained in product development can be amplified by improving how teams collaborate and manage projects using AI tools. Businesses can ensure that the ideas generated during the ideation phase are brought to market efficiently by enhancing team collaboration. In the next chapter, we will discuss the role of AI in team collaboration and project management. We will discuss how AI tools can improve communication, task management, and productivity.

9. Team Collaboration and Project Management

Team collaboration and project management are important for business success. Teams are becoming more diverse and distributed, and the need for solutions to enhance collaboration and optimize project workflows has never been greater.

As businesses strive to float, more and more are turning to artificial intelligence (AI) to optimize their team's performance and project outcomes. A recent survey by beautiful.ai indicates that 95% of managers already utilize AI tools to heighten productivity levels within their teams. This shows how important AI tools are and will be in a few years to come.

However, we will explore how AI and ChatGPT can help improve team collaboration and optimize project management processes. From streamlining workflows to improving communication and ensuring projects are completed efficiently and effectively, these tools are helping teams work together to achieve their goals.

AI's Role in Facilitating Team Collaboration

Building strong teams requires more than just individual skills —it demands effective communication, collaboration, and cohesion. However, achieving this can be challenging, especially in diverse or remote teams. ChatGPT can help teams overcome communication barriers by providing real-time language translation to enable seamless interaction among team members who speak different languages. This capability promotes inclusivity and ensures that everyone's voice is heard, regardless of their linguistic background.

ChatGPT also enhances remote collaboration by acting as a virtual meeting assistant. It can help generate agendas and even provide summaries, making it easier for team members to collaborate effectively across different time zones and locations. Decision-making becomes easier with AI tools. It can improve the decision-making process within teams by analyzing data, providing useful information, and offering recommendations. This enables teams to make informed decisions on time, leading to more efficient workflows and better outcomes.

They say, "Knowledge is power." AI tools can help in facilitating knowledge sharing by acting as a repository of information. Team members can ask ChatGPT for information on specific topics or processes, helping to disseminate knowledge and best practices across the team.

Benefits of AI-Powered Collaboration Tools

The way we work is constantly changing, and collaboration is more important than ever before. However, old methods of teamwork can be hindered by communication barriers, geographical separation, and repetitive tasks. AI-powered collaboration tools offer many benefits to improve the ideation process, help team members, and promote creativity. Here are some benefits:

Boosting the Ideation Process with AI Generation

AI tools are great for sparking new ideas and overcoming creative roadblocks. It can generate variations on existing concepts or even create visual prototypes based on preliminary ideas. This infuses fresh perspectives into the process, encouraging teams to think outside the box and explore new possibilities. For instance, AI can generate basic wireframes for web applications, create rough drafts of marketing copy, or even develop simple 3D models based on team descriptions. This allows teams to test and refine concepts without needing extensive technical expertise, leading to faster decision-making.

Empowering Team Members through Automation

Many collaboration tools incorporate AI-powered automation features that can handle repetitive tasks such as scheduling meetings, taking notes, generating reports, or managing data. It allows time for team members to focus on higher-level cognitive tasks like strategic planning, creative problem-solving, and building strong relationships with colleagues. AI can also analyze team communication patterns and identify areas where individual members might benefit from additional training or skill development. This allows for personalized learning recommendations to ensure that each team member is equipped with the necessary skills and knowledge to contribute effectively.

Enhancing Engagement and Fostering Creativity

AI tools can analyze communication patterns and sieve out potential conflicts or areas of tension within a team for early intervention and proactive measures to address issues before they escalate. It can analyze communication styles and tailor its interactions as required. This can be particularly helpful for managing remote teams or working with individuals from diverse backgrounds. Certain AI tools can incorporate gamification elements into the collaboration process to make tasks more engaging and encourage friendly competition among team members.

Reducing Time Wasting

Misunderstandings and a lack of clarity can waste significant time in team settings. AI tools can translate languages and summarize complex information into clear takeaways. This ensures everyone is on the same page, eliminates the need for repetitive clarification requests, and allows for a smoother communication flow. It can also be used to automate the creation and assignment of action items following meetings or discussions.

This provides a clear record of the next steps, removes the ambiguity of "who's responsible for what," and allows for easy tracking of progress. With clear ownership and automated reminders, your team members can hold each other accountable.

Providing Clarity on Next Steps

AI-powered project management tools can provide daily insights into project progress, identify potential roadblocks, and suggest alternative courses of action. This allows for proactive decision-making and ensures that teams are always aware of the necessary steps and adjustments. It can also analyze meeting recordings or transcripts and generate summaries that highlight key decisions, action items, and deadlines to ensure everyone has a clear understanding of the next steps and eliminate the need for lengthy recap emails or follow-up meetings. With clear and concise summaries, teams can quickly get back to work without wasting time trying to piece together the details of previous discussions.

Strengthening Human Skills

Some AI tools can analyze team communication patterns and check for areas where individual members might benefit from additional training or skill development. This allows for the creation of personalized learning pathways, ensuring that everyone on the team continues to develop their skills and contribute to their full potential. It can also suggest targeted resources, helping your team become better collaborators.

Also, by automating repetitive tasks, AI frees up brainpower for teams to focus on higher-level tasks that involve creative problem-solving and developing solutions. You no longer spend hours on administrative tasks but can dedicate that time to developing long-term plans.

Balancing Workloads and Working Hours

With AI tools, you can analyze team skill sets, workload capacity, and project deadlines. This allows for intelligent task distribution so that tasks are assigned to the most suitable team member based on their expertise and current workload. This optimizes project outcomes and prevents situations where certain individuals are overloaded while others are underutilized.

It can use historical data and project requirements to predict potential workload bottlenecks to allow for proactive workload management, enabling teams to adjust project timelines, delegate tasks strategically, or even use opportunities for automation to prevent burnout.

Promoting Independence and Confidence

You can use AI tools to analyze team communication patterns and look out for areas where individual members might benefit from additional training or skill development. These insights can be used to curate personalized learning recommendations, which help you focus on areas that will enhance your skills and contribute more effectively to the team. AI tools that act as virtual mentors can give feedback on tasks, suggest best practices, and give guidance on overcoming challenges. This support helps you tackle tasks independently, promoting a sense of self-reliance and boosting confidence in your abilities.

ChatGPT Prompts for Team Collaboration

Here are twenty ChatGPT prompts you can try as a team to improve collaboration and communication patterns:

- **Brainstorming Boost**: We are facing a creative block on (project name). Generate ten unexpected ideas related to (key challenge) to spark a brainstorming session.
- **Meeting Magician**: Craft an engaging agenda for a (meeting type) meeting focused on (meeting objective). Include discussion prompts and icebreaker activities for a geographically dispersed team.
- **Task Delegation Dynamo**: Considering team skill sets and the current workload, suggest an optimal way to distribute tasks for the upcoming (project name) project.
- **Knowledge Navigator**: Our team is working on (topic). Generate a concise summary of the key points and insights from the top three relevant research articles.
- **Action Item Architect**: Based on our meeting

discussion, create a clear and actionable list of the next steps with assigned owners and deadlines for each task.

- **Meeting Recap Maestro**: Summarize the key decisions and action items from our recent meeting on (topic) in a clear and concise format for easy reference. (Provide ChatGPT with the details of the meeting.)
- **Conflict Calmer**: Two team members seem to have differing viewpoints on (issue). Generate a list of open-ended questions to facilitate a productive and respectful discussion.
- **Feedback Facilitator**: We are conducting peer reviews for (project type). Craft a set of unbiased questions to guide team members in providing constructive and actionable feedback.
- **Icebreaker Improviser**: The team is feeling a bit disconnected working remotely. Suggest a fun and engaging virtual icebreaker activity to promote team bonding.
- **Presentation Polisher**: We are finalizing a presentation for (audience). Analyze the content and suggest improvements for clarity, flow, and audience engagement. (Provide ChatGPT with the content.)
- **Diversity and Inclusion Detective:** Review our current team communication style and identify potential areas where we can improve inclusivity for diverse team members. (Provide ChatGPT with details on the communication style.)
- **Meeting Minutes Marvel**: "Based on the audio recording of our meeting, generate a comprehensive set of meeting minutes with timestamps for key points.

- **Gamification Guru**: We are looking for ways to make our weekly team meetings more engaging. Suggest a gamified approach that incentivizes participation and knowledge sharing.
- **Brainstorming Buddy**: We need to develop a marketing strategy for (product/service). Generate a mind map outlining potential target audiences, messaging ideas, and promotional channels.
- **Decision-Making Dynamo**: The team is divided (decision point). Analyze the pros and cons of each option based on available data and suggest a data-driven approach to reach a consensus.
- **Project Planner Pro**: Outline a detailed project plan for (project name), including milestones, deadlines, resource allocation, and potential risk factors.
- **Meeting Mood Meter**: Analyze the sentiment of our last team meeting based on transcripts. Identify areas for improvement in fostering a positive and collaborative atmosphere.
- **Knowledge Repository**: Create a searchable knowledge base for our team, summarizing key takeaways from past projects, best practices documents, and frequently asked questions.
- **Meeting Role Randomizer**: We typically have the same team members take on specific roles in meetings. Randomly assign roles (facilitator, timekeeper, and notetaker) for the next meeting to encourage participation from all members.
- **Teamwork Translator**: Our team includes members from different cultural backgrounds. Help us identify

potential communication gaps and suggest strategies for effective cross-cultural collaboration.

Using AI for Project Management Optimization

Project management is a delicate dance—juggling tasks, resources, and deadlines while keeping everything on track. However, with artificial intelligence (AI), you can optimize every stage of the project lifecycle, from planning and execution to monitoring and completion. Here's how AI helps in project management:

- **Planning with Foresight:** No more endless spreadsheets and manual calculations. AI can analyze historical project data, including task durations, resource dependencies, and potential roadblocks. This allows it to generate intelligent and realistic project schedules to help you start your project on the right foot.

- **Resource Allocation Redefined:** You no longer need to do guesswork about who should be assigned to which task. AI takes your team's strengths, skills, and current workloads into account to make optimal resource allocation. The right person gets the right job at the right time, every time.

- **Risk Management on Autopilot:** Project risks are like uninvited guests at a party—they can derail everything. AI acts as your security guard to analyze past project data and predict potential risks before they crash the party. It will then suggest preventative measures and contingency plans to be prepared for the unexpected.

- **Automating the Mundane:** Let AI handle the repetitive tasks that bog down your team, like automatic progress reports, scheduling meetings, and data entry. This task automation allows your team to have valuable time and mental space for more strategic work and to focus on what truly matters.

- **Real-Time Progress Tracking:** Gone are the days of scrambling for updates. AI provides live project monitoring, gathering data from various sources and presenting a clear picture of your project's progress. It does this by analyzing your data in real-time, spotting risks and roadblocks before they become disasters, and then predicting future issues based on past projects and current trends for proactive solutions. Tools like Otus can give off alerts to warn of potential problems, while ChatGPT helps generate reports and suggest solutions to keep everyone informed.

- **Predictive Power for Course Correction:** AI is your proactive partner. It processes progress data and singles out potential deviations from the plan. Before minor issues creep into major problems, it will suggest course corrections or resource adjustments so your project stays on track.

- **Communication and Collaboration on Steroids:** Communication breakdowns can cripple a project. Different AI tools can step in as your communication facilitator, automatically generating status reports with ChatGPT, distributing task updates with Trello, and translating languages with EdApp. This promotes collaboration within your team and ensures that everyone is on the same page all the time.

- **Data-Driven Decisions, Every Time:** Stop relying on gut feelings. AI helps you make informed decisions accurately and effectively with its data-driven insights. Real-time data and project performance metrics will help guide your choices for better outcomes.
- **Reduced Costs and Boosted Efficiency:** Optimizing resource allocation, automating mundane tasks, and minimizing rework through risk mitigation—these all add up to one thing: reduced project costs. This translates to increased efficiency across the board and a significant productivity boost for your team.

ChatGPT Prompts for Project Management

Here are a few ChatGPT prompts to boost project management:

- **Project Kickoff Canvas**: We are kicking off a new project called (project name). Generate a comprehensive project charter outlining goals, stakeholders, deadlines, and success metrics.
- **WBS Wizard**: Help us create a detailed Work Breakdown Structure (WBS) for (project name), breaking down the project into manageable tasks and subtasks.
- **Schedule Sensei**: Based on task dependencies and resource availability, create a realistic project schedule

using Gantt chart format, highlighting critical paths and potential milestones.

- **Risk Radar**: Identify the top five potential risks associated with (project name) and suggest corresponding mitigation strategies for each.
- **Budget Blueprint**: Develop a comprehensive project budget outlining estimated costs for labor, materials, and any potential contingencies.
- **Communication Calendar Composer**: Craft a communication plan for (project name) that outlines communication channels, frequency, and key information to be shared with stakeholders.
- **Meeting**: Generate an engaging agenda for a project kickoff meeting, including introductions, project overview, and opportunities for team members to ask questions.
- **Meeting Minutes**: Summarize the key decisions, action items, and next steps from our recent project meeting on (topic) in a clear and concise format for easy reference.
- **Progress Tracker Pro**: Provide tips to design a user-friendly dashboard to track project progress visually, including key metrics like task completion rates, budget adherence, and deadline milestones. (Use ChatGPT premium.)
- **Collaboration Catalyst**: The team seems to be struggling with collaboration on a specific task. Suggest strategies and tools to improve communication and information sharing within the team.

- **Issue Identifier**: Analyze project data and identify potential roadblocks or areas where the project is falling behind schedule.
- **Change Management Champion**: We need to communicate a significant change to the project scope with stakeholders. Craft a clear and concise message that outlines the rationale for the change and its impact on the project.
- **Meeting Energizer**: The team's energy seems low during project meetings. Engaging activities or icebreakers are recommended to boost morale and participation.
- **Lessons Learned Log**: Help us capture key takeaways and lessons learned from (project name) to inform future project management decisions.
- **Risk Re-Assessment Radar**: The project has progressed significantly since the initial risk assessment. Re-evaluate potential risks and adjust mitigation strategies accordingly.
- **Budget Variance Analyst**: Project costs are exceeding the original budget. Analyze the reasons for the variance and suggest cost-saving measures to stay within budget.
- **Stakeholder Satisfaction Surveyor**: Develop a survey to collect feedback from stakeholders on their satisfaction with the project's progress and communication.
- **Project Post-Mortem Mastermind**: Facilitate a team discussion to analyze the successes and challenges of

(project name). Identify areas for improvement for future projects.

- **Teamwork Trainer**: The project team is encountering communication challenges due to cultural differences. Recommend strategies and resources to foster a more inclusive and collaborative team environment.

Wrap-Up

While AI offers tremendous benefits for team collaboration and project management, it is important to acknowledge the ethical and privacy concerns that come with its implementation. Businesses are embracing AI technologies to improve productivity and efficiency, but they must also be aware of ethical considerations surrounding data privacy, algorithm bias, and transparency. The next chapter will look into these critical issues, guiding ethical AI use and data protection. Addressing these concerns will help to ensure that AI initiatives align with ethical principles and respect the rights and privacy of individuals.

10. Ethics, Privacy, and the Future

As AI becomes a staple in business, 90% of shoppers believe retailers should be required to openly disclose how they use customer data in applying AI usage (TalkDesk Stats). This striking statement gives a glimpse into a growing awareness and concern among consumers regarding the ethical implications of AI integration in business operations. AI technologies, especially ChatGPT, are becoming increasingly popular, and businesses need to understand the principles of ethics and privacy.

Businesses that continue to use AI in their daily operations must answer questions of transparency, fairness, and accountability. How should AI algorithms be trained and deployed to minimize bias and discrimination? What measures should be put in place to protect consumer privacy and data security in an increasingly connected world? These are just a few of the pressing ethical considerations that businesses must address as they leverage AI technology.

Also, staying abreast of future ethical directions and regulatory expectations is important to maintain trust and credibility with consumers and stakeholders. This chapter will confront the ethical dilemmas and privacy challenges posed by the integration of AI and ChatGPT in business operations. It will equip you with the knowledge and tools needed to implement AI solutions responsibly, safeguard data privacy, and adhere to ethical standards.

Understanding Ethical Considerations

AI offers much potential for improving efficiency and decision-making in the workplace; however, its implementation raises critical questions about responsible and ethical use. Ethical AI goes beyond simply complying with legal regulations. It's about establishing a strong ethical framework that guides the development, deployment, and use of AI within a business. This framework centers around core values that ensure AI benefits society and avoids causing harm. Here's a breakdown of some key ethical considerations for businesses:

- **Nondiscrimination:** AI algorithms can perpetuate biases present in the data they are trained on. This can lead to discriminatory outcomes in areas like hiring, loan approvals, or even facial recognition software. Businesses must ensure their AI is developed and used in a way that treats everyone fairly and avoids perpetuating existing societal inequalities.

- **Privacy:** AI systems often rely on data, raising concerns about user privacy. Businesses must be transparent about how they collect, store, and use customer data. They also need safeguards in place to prevent unauthorized access or misuse of personal information.
- **Individual Rights:** The increasing use of AI in decision-making processes can raise concerns about individual rights. For instance, AI-powered hiring algorithms could unfairly disadvantage certain candidates. Businesses need to ensure individuals have the right to understand how AI is being used to make decisions about them and have avenues to appeal or rectify any potential biases.
- **Nonmanipulation:** AI can be used for manipulative purposes, such as creating deepfakes or crafting targeted advertising that exploits user vulnerabilities. Businesses must ensure their AI is used responsibly and ethically, avoiding practices that deceive or manipulate consumers.

Why Prioritize Ethical AI?

Why prioritizing ethical AI goes beyond just being the "right thing to do":

- **Reduces Risk:** Unethical AI practices can lead to legal repercussions, reputational damage, and consumer backlash. Businesses that proactively address ethical considerations can mitigate these risks.

- **Builds Trust:** Consumers are increasingly concerned about how their data is used. You can build trust with customers, employees, and stakeholders by demonstrating a commitment to ethical AI practices. This promotes a positive brand image and leads to a competitive advantage.
- **Sustainable Growth:** Long-term success hinges on responsible AI development and use. Ethical AI ensures that AI technology benefits all of society, not just a select few, and that it aligns with positive societal values, contributing to a responsible and ethical future.

How to Operationalize Data and AI Ethics

Operationalizing data and AI ethics requires a multi-faceted approach that goes beyond having good intentions. Here's a breakdown of key steps to translate ethical principles into concrete actions within your organization:

Establish a Strong Foundation

The AI framework should clearly outline your organization's values and principles regarding data and AI use. It should address issues like fairness, transparency, accountability, and privacy. Organize training sessions and workshops to educate employees about ethical considerations surrounding data and AI. This builds a culture of ethical responsibility and helps employees flag potential issues.

Integrate Ethics into the AI Lifecycle

Clearly define the purpose of data collection, ensure user consent, and establish procedures for data anonymization and security. You should also scrutinize the data used to train AI models to mitigate potential biases while employing techniques like fairness checks and bias mitigation algorithms to ensure fair and nondiscriminatory outcomes. Continuously monitor the performance of deployed AI models to detect and address any unintended consequences or biases that may occur over time.

Promote Transparency and Accountability

Whenever possible, strive to develop AI models that are explainable and interpretable. This allows humans to understand how the AI arrives at its decisions and potential biases. Also, consider offering users the right to request an explanation for AI-driven decisions that impact them to promote trust and allow for potential redress if an AI decision seems unfair. Regular auditing and reporting are also important; conduct regular audits to assess your organization's adherence to ethical AI principles and develop clear reporting mechanisms to communicate ethical considerations and potential risks to stakeholders.

Embrace Continuous Improvement

The regulatory landscape surrounding AI is changing every day. You should stay up-to-date on new regulations, adapt your practices accordingly, and encourage open communication within your organization about ethical concerns related to data and AI. Provide clear channels for employees to report potential issues without fear of reprisal and actively participate in industry discussions while collaborating with other organizations to share best practices and learn from each other's experiences in operationalizing data and AI ethics.

Common Ethical Concerns Related to AI

Here are common ethical concerns businesses should look for when using AI:

Unjustified Actions

One of the primary ethical concerns with AI is the potential for unjustified actions or decisions. AI systems, particularly those based on machine learning algorithms, make decisions based on patterns in data. However, these decisions may not always align with ethical or moral principles. For example, an AI-powered recruitment system may mistakenly discriminate against certain demographics, leading to unfair hiring practices. Unjustified actions can also arise when AI systems lack proper oversight or fail to consider the broader societal implications of their decisions.

Opacity

Opacity refers to the lack of transparency and explainability in AI systems. Many AI algorithms operate as "black boxes," meaning that their decision-making processes are not easily understandable or explainable to humans. This lack of transparency can lead to distrust and uncertainty, especially when AI systems are used in critical applications such as healthcare or criminal justice. Without transparency, it's challenging to address biases or errors in AI systems, potentially causing unintended consequences or harm.

Bias

Bias in AI systems occurs when the algorithms produce results that systematically favor or disadvantage certain groups of people. It can arise from various sources, including biased training data, flawed algorithms, or unintentional biases in the design or implementation of AI systems. If historical data used to train a predictive policing algorithm reflects existing biases in law enforcement practices, the algorithm may perpetuate or even exacerbate these biases. Bias in AI systems can lead to unfair treatment, discrimination, and social inequality.

Discrimination

Discrimination is the risk of AI systems exhibiting bias or making decisions that disproportionately impact certain individuals or groups based on factors such as race, gender, age, or socioeconomic status. This bias can arise from prejudiced training data or unintended correlations in the data. Discriminatory AI systems can perpetuate or worsen existing societal inequalities and injustices.

To address this concern, it is important to implement measures to mitigate bias in AI systems. This includes using diverse and representative training data, conducting bias assessments and audits, and developing fairness-aware algorithms that prioritize equitable outcomes. Also, transparency and accountability mechanisms should be in place to ensure that AI decisions are explainable and auditable.

Autonomy

The increasing autonomy of AI systems raises ethical concerns regarding accountability, responsibility, and control. As AI systems become more autonomous and capable of making decisions without human intervention, questions arise about who should be held accountable for the actions and decisions of these systems. There is also concern about the potential loss of human agency and control over AI systems, especially in critical domains such as healthcare, criminal justice, and autonomous vehicles.

To address these concerns, there is a need to establish clear lines of accountability and responsibility for AI systems. This includes defining the roles and responsibilities of developers, operators, and users of AI systems and establishing mechanisms for oversight, transparency, and recourse in case of errors or failures. Also, human oversight and intervention should be incorporated into AI systems to ensure that they operate within ethical and legal boundaries.

Informational Privacy and Group Privacy

Informational privacy refers to the right of individuals to control their data and how it is collected, used, and shared by AI systems. Ethical concerns arise when AI systems collect and process large amounts of personal data without individuals' consent or awareness, causing privacy breaches, surveillance, and exploitation.

To protect informational and group privacy, businesses must enforce data protection measures and privacy-enhancing technologies. This includes obtaining informed consent from individuals for data collection and processing, implementing data anonymization and encryption techniques to protect sensitive information, and establishing clear data governance policies and procedures. Also, regulatory frameworks such as the General Data Protection Regulation (GDPR) provide guidelines for the responsible use of personal data and impose penalties for noncompliance.

Moral Responsibility and Distributed Responsibility

Another major ethical concern is the allocation of moral responsibility for the actions of AI systems. As AI becomes more independent, questions regarding who should be held accountable for the decisions and actions of AI systems should be discussed. This concept of "distributed responsibility" challenges traditional notions of accountability and raises questions about the ethical implications of AI systems acting independently of human control.

Automation Bias

Automation bias refers to the tendency of individuals to favor information or decisions made by automated systems, even when they conflict with their judgment or expertise. This can lead to over-reliance on AI systems, causing errors or ethical issues. Addressing automation bias requires careful consideration of how AI systems are designed and implemented to ensure that they augment human decision-making rather than replace it entirely.

Safety and Resilience

Safety and resilience are important ethical concerns in high-stakes domains such as healthcare, autonomous vehicles, and finance. Ensuring the safety of AI systems involves designing rugged systems that can detect and recover from errors or unexpected situations. Also, ethical considerations around safety include minimizing the potential harm caused by AI systems and ensuring that they do not pose a risk to individuals or society.

Ethical Auditing

Ethical auditing involves assessing the ethical implications of AI systems throughout their lifecycle. This includes evaluating the design, development, deployment, and use of AI systems to ensure that they align with ethical principles and values. Ethical auditing helps point out and mitigate potential ethical risks associated with AI systems and ensures that they are used in a responsible and ethical manner.

Addressing Privacy Concerns in AI

The use of AI presents significant privacy implications due to its remarkable capacity to analyze data. AI algorithms process data from various sources, including personal information, and infer sensitive information about individuals, such as their location, preferences, habits, and even health status. For instance, AI systems can analyze browsing history, social media activity, and online purchases to make predictions about an individual's interests, behavior, and lifestyle. This capability raises concerns about the privacy of personal data and the potential for unauthorized access or misuse.

The use of AI increases the risk of unauthorized data distribution, where sensitive information is shared or accessed without consent. AI systems may disclose personal data through data breaches, hacking attacks, or unauthorized access by third parties. This can lead to privacy violations, identity theft, and other forms of harm to individuals. It can also manipulate personal data to create detailed profiles of individuals, increasing the risk of theft and fraud. Cybercriminals can use AI to automate the process of gathering and analyzing personal information, making it easier to impersonate individuals or access their accounts. This poses a significant threat to individuals' privacy and security.

Also, AI-powered surveillance systems can monitor individuals' activities in public spaces, workplaces, and online environments, leading to increased scrutiny and violations of privacy rights. Moreover, the deployment of facial recognition technology and other biometric identification systems raises concerns about mass surveillance and the reduction in privacy.

Best Practices for Data Privacy When Using AI

As the use of AI continues to become prevalent among industries, ensuring data privacy remains an important aspect of its use. However, here's a breakdown of best practices for data governance when implementing AI solutions:

Understanding AI Laws and Regulation

Research and understand relevant regional and national data privacy regulations, such as GDPR (General Data Protection Regulation) and CCPA (California Consumer Privacy Act). These regulations outline guidelines for data collection, storage, usage, and user consent. Familiarize yourself with relevant regulations applicable to your location and industry. Consult with legal professionals specializing in data privacy to ensure your AI practices comply with current regulations. They can advise on specific steps to take to mitigate legal risks.

Establishing a Data Governance Framework

Develop a clear framework outlining data collection practices for AI applications. This includes obtaining informed user consent, minimizing data collection to vital elements, and adhering to data minimization principles. Whenever possible, anonymize data to protect individual identities. Use techniques like differential privacy that use only the minimum data points necessary for AI functionality.

Make privacy concerns important and implement cybersecurity protocols to safeguard sensitive data. This includes encryption techniques, access controls, and regular security audits. You also need to define your data retention policies, outlining how long data is stored and the procedures for secure disposal after its designated purpose is fulfilled.

Assessing Ethical Implications

Thoroughly assess the ethical implications of AI technologies before deployment. Consider potential biases in the training data and how the AI might affect individuals or groups. You should also integrate diverse perspectives into the development process. This includes ethicists, lawyers, and individuals from varied backgrounds to ensure inclusive AI development.

Providing Transparency and Awareness

Be transparent about how user data is collected, used, and shared for AI applications, and give clear and accessible privacy policies that users can understand. You should also offer users control over their data by providing the right to access, rectify, or erase their data upon request.

Conduct a Privacy Impact Assessment (PIA)

Before deploying any AI system, a privacy impact assessment (PIA) is essential. This approach helps pinpoint likely privacy risks. A PIA involves identifying all the data points collected, how they are used by the AI system, and with whom they might be shared, analyzing the risks associated with each data point, and formulating strategies to minimize the impact of each specified risk. This might involve anonymization techniques, data minimization practices, or enforcing security measures.

Implement Data Retention and Minimization Policies

Data collection for AI applications should be a targeted exercise. The principle of data minimization dictates that only the data essential for the AI's functionality should be collected. Avoid collecting extraneous information that doesn't directly contribute to the AI's purpose. Establish clear guidelines on how long data is stored. Once the data has fulfilled its purpose for the AI system, it should be securely disposed of following established protocols.

Introduce Robust Data Security Measures

Since AI systems often handle sensitive data, cybersecurity measures are paramount. Implement encryption techniques to protect data at rest and in transit, reducing the risk of unauthorized access in the event of a breach. You also need to establish clear access control protocols, granting access to data only to authorized personnel who require it for their specific roles.

Conduct regular security audits to check for vulnerabilities in your systems and execute necessary security patches promptly.

Develop a Breach Response Plan

Despite the best precautions, data breaches can still occur. Having a well-defined breach response plan in place helps you deal with such situations better. You should start by establishing procedures for promptly detecting a data breach and reporting it to the relevant authorities and affected individuals, as mandated by law. Develop strategies to contain the breach, minimize damage, and remediate the vulnerability that led to the incident, and define a clear communication strategy for informing affected individuals and stakeholders about the breach, its impact, and the steps being taken to address it.

Guidelines for Responsible AI Implementation

The use of AI goes hand-in-hand with a great responsibility: ensuring its ethical and responsible use. This guide provides a roadmap for businesses to understand AI ethical implementation, promote trust, and achieve long-term success.

Anchoring AI in Ethical Values

A strong ethical framework is the cornerstone of responsible AI. Here's how to establish one:

- **Identify Core Values:** Define the core values that will guide your organization's AI development and use.

These values should reflect your commitment to fairness, transparency, privacy, and accountability. Examples include nondiscrimination, data security, and human oversight.

- **Develop AI Principles:** Translate your core values into specific AI principles. This could include ensuring unbiased decision-making, respecting user privacy, and maintaining human control over AI systems.
- **Embed AI Principles in Culture:** Integrate your AI principles into your company culture. Educate employees about ethical AI practices and create an environment where responsible AI development is championed.

Establishing Accountability through Structure

Clear lines of responsibility are important for ethical AI. Here's how to achieve that:

- **Form an AI Governance Board:** Create a dedicated body responsible for overseeing the ethical development and deployment of AI within your organization. This board should include representatives from various departments (engineering, legal, ethics, etc.) for a well-rounded perspective.
- **Define Roles and Responsibilities:** Clearly define roles and responsibilities for all stakeholders involved in AI development and use. This includes data scientists, engineers, project managers, and executives.

Everyone should understand their part in maintaining ethical principles.

- **Implement Oversight Mechanisms:** Establish clear oversight mechanisms to monitor AI systems for potential biases, fairness issues, and security vulnerabilities. Regular audits and reporting can help address problems faster.

Mitigating Risk and Building Resilience

AI systems are not without risks. Here's how to curb them:

- **Conduct Bias Audits:** Regularly assess your AI systems for potential biases in the data, algorithms, and decision-making processes. Identify and address any biases found through bias mitigation techniques or data cleansing.
- **Prioritize Data Privacy:** Implement data security measures to protect user privacy and ensure data is collected and used in accordance with ethical guidelines and regulations (refer to data privacy best practices for specifics).
- **Build Explainable AI Systems:** Strive to create AI systems that are transparent and explainable. This allows for human oversight and intervention when necessary. Explainable AI techniques can help understand how AI arrives at decisions.
- **Develop Robust Testing Processes:** Implement thorough testing procedures throughout the AI development lifecycle to recognize and address possible

risks and vulnerabilities before deployment. Testing should include edge cases and real-world scenarios.

Detecting and Remediating Bias

AI systems are susceptible to biases that can lead to unfair or discriminatory outcomes. Here's how to combat them:

- **Identify Biases in Data:** Analyze your data sets for potential biases. Look for imbalances in demographics, historical trends, or how data is collected. Consider using bias detection tools like IBM AI Fairness 360, Microsoft's Fairlearn, and What-If Tool to help identify potential issues.
- **De-bias Training Data:** If biases are found in your training data, take steps to reduce them. This could involve data augmentation (adding data points to underrepresented groups) or data cleansing (removing biased data).
- **Fairness Testing:** Incorporate fairness testing throughout the AI development lifecycle. Test your AI system against diverse datasets to ensure it delivers fair and unbiased results across different demographics.

Ensuring Human Oversight

AI is powerful, but it shouldn't replace human judgment entirely. Here's why human oversight matters:

- **Ethical Decision-Making:** Humans can provide crucial ethical considerations that AI systems may lack. Maintain human oversight for pressing decisions made by AI systems, especially those with more social or legal implications.
- **Accountability and Transparency:** Human oversight ensures clear lines of accountability. If an AI system makes a mistake, it's clear who is responsible for addressing it.
- **Maintaining Control:** Humans should maintain control over AI systems to ensure they are used for their intended purposes and can be deactivated or adjusted if necessary.

Ensuring Transparency and Explainability

Without understanding how AI systems arrive at their decisions, it's difficult to trust them. Here's how to promote transparency:

- **Explainable AI (XAI) Techniques:** Use XAI techniques to make AI decision-making processes more transparent. This allows humans to understand the factors influencing the AI's outputs.
- **Documenting AI Development:** Maintain clear documentation of the AI development process, including data selection, algorithm design, and testing procedures. This transparency builds trust and facilitates future audits.

- **Communicating with Stakeholders:** Communicate how AI systems work to stakeholders, including users, regulators, and the public. Explain the limitations of AI and the safeguards in place to reduce risks.

How to Educate Your Employees Involved in AI Development and Deployment

Integrating AI successfully into your business requires not just technology but also a workforce equipped with the knowledge and skills to use AI responsibly and effectively. Let's look at ways you can educate your employees on the right implementation of AI.

Establishing an AI Usage Policy

Develop a comprehensive AI usage policy that outlines your organization's commitment to ethical AI principles. This policy should cover data privacy, bias mitigation, human oversight, and transparency. You should also communicate the AI usage policy widely throughout your organization. Organize town halls, Q&A sessions, or internal communication campaigns to ensure all employees understand the policy and its implications.

Providing Ethical AI Training

Go beyond traditional lectures. Combine interactive elements like case studies, simulations, and role-playing exercises to make learning engaging and practical. Develop training programs specific to different employee roles. For example, engineers might need in-depth training on bias detection in data sets, while marketing personnel might benefit from understanding how AI can be used ethically in customer interactions. Make this an ongoing process. Integrating AI training modules into existing learning and development programs can help ensure employees stay up-to-date with the latest advancements and best practices.

Building Organizational and Departmental Plans

Appoint AI champions within each department. These champions can act as internal resources, answering questions, providing guidance, and promoting ethical AI practices among their colleagues. Work with each department to create specific plans for integrating AI into their workflows. These plans should consider ethical considerations, potential risks, and solution strategies. Also, cross-departmental collaboration on AI projects should be encouraged. This promotes knowledge sharing and ensures a holistic approach to ethical AI implementation across the organization.

Training Employees on Effective AI Use

Don't just teach the theory behind AI. Train employees on how to use AI tools in their specific roles. This could include data analysis techniques, model interpretation, or responsible AI communication strategies. Encourage employees to ask questions, raise concerns, and report possible ethical issues related to AI while creating a safe space for open dialogue about responsible AI implementation.

Setting Goals and Optimizing

Set clear learning objectives for your AI education programs. This helps measure the effectiveness of your training and specify areas for improvement. Gather feedback from employees, adjust your training strategies based on their needs and the AI landscape, and embrace a culture of continuous improvement in your AI education efforts. As AI technologies and regulations expand, so, too, should your approach to employee training.

Future Trends

AI is constantly growing with daily improvements in its capabilities. Here, we will explore some of the most exciting trends that promise to reshape our interactions with technology and the world around us:

Beyond the Keyboard: The Rise of Voice-Centric AI

Text-based interfaces are becoming a thing of the past. With NLP, expect AI to become more adept at understanding the nuances of human speech, accents, and slang. Seamless voice interactions will become the norm, adjusting how we search for information, control smart devices, and interact with digital assistants. It can act as a personal trainer guiding you through a workout routine with voice commands or a doctor conducting a virtual consultation entirely through voice interaction.

Breaking the Modality Barrier

AI is no longer confined to a single data type—the future is multimodal. AI models are being trained to process information from different sources at the same time. Multimodal AI will create richer and more intuitive user experiences. For example, an AI assistant might use a combination of voice commands, facial recognition, and contextual awareness to predict your needs and offer help.

AI Planners

AI can become your ultimate productivity tool. It will automate more than just repetitive tasks. Expect AI planners to suggest relevant articles to read based on your interests, schedule meetings with the right people, or even book travel arrangements based on your preferences and budget. It will analyze your emails, calendar appointments, and even weather forecasts to suggest the most efficient schedule for your day. AI planners will learn your preferences and adjust schedules to stay on top of your tasks.

The Rise of Autonomous Agents

AI assistants are taking on a life of their own—in a good way. Autonomous AI agents won't just wait for instructions. They will proactively monitor situations, identify potential problems, and suggest solutions before they escalate. This could help in areas like network security or industrial process management. AI agents will be able to navigate a physical environment, interact with objects, and complete tasks independently. This paves the way for robots that can perform tasks in dangerous environments, assist with elderly care, or even provide companionship.

Vector Databases and Embeddings

Behind the scenes, the way AI processes information is undergoing a transformation. These databases store information as vectors (multidimensional points) in a high-dimensional space. This allows AI to identify relationships and similarities between data points more subtly. The process of transforming data (text, images, etc.) into vectors is known as embedding. Vector databases and embeddings will play a vital role in enabling AI to perform complex tasks like natural language translation, image recognition, and recommendation systems.

How to Stay Ahead with AI News

The world of AI is a fast-paced one. New developments and breakthroughs seem to arise daily. But fear not, here are some helpful tips to ensure you stay informed and updated on the latest AI news and trends:

Follow the Right Online Resources

Subscribe to newsletters from reputable AI news sources. These newsletters will deliver the latest headlines and information straight to your inbox. You can also check out prominent AI blogs and websites like MIT Technology Review, AI Today, and VentureBeat. These platforms offer in-depth articles, interviews with experts, and analysis of the latest advancements. Join AI-focused groups on LinkedIn, Reddit, or Facebook. These groups promote discussions, allow you to connect with other AI enthusiasts, and provide access to shared resources.

Attend Events and Webinars

Engage yourself in the AI community by attending industry conferences and workshops. These events offer opportunities to learn from leading experts, network with peers, and discover emerging trends firsthand. Many organizations and institutions host free or paid webinars on various AI topics. Take advantage of these online learning opportunities to broaden your knowledge base.

Sharpen Your Skill Set

Enroll in online courses offered by platforms like Coursera, edX, or Udacity. These courses can teach you valuable skills in AI, machine learning, data science, or specific AI applications relevant to your field. Consider intensive coding boot camps to gain hands-on experience with AI tools and libraries. Learning to code will help you understand AI and potentially build your own AI applications.

Network with Peers and Experts

Follow prominent AI researchers, developers, and thought leaders on social media platforms like Twitter or LinkedIn. Engage in discussions, ask questions, and learn from their insights. Look for local AI meetups or events in your area. These gatherings provide a platform to connect with other AI enthusiasts, share knowledge, and collaborate on potential projects.

Experiment and Innovate

The best way to truly understand AI is to get your hands dirty. Explore open-source AI tools and experiment with building your own small-scale AI projects. This practical experience will solidify your understanding and spark your creativity. Consider contributing to open-source AI projects to allow you to learn from experienced developers, stay at the forefront of inventions, and give back to the AI community.

Embrace Curiosity and Open-Mindedness

The key to staying ahead in AI is a genuine curiosity about the technology and its prospects. Ask questions, explore diverse perspectives, and challenge your assumptions. The field of AI is constantly growing; be open to new ideas, technologies, and the impact of AI on various aspects of life.

Wrap-Up

We have explored the potential of AI for optimizing productivity, from planning and execution to monitoring and completion. However, this comes with a responsibility—ensuring the ethical and responsible development and implementation of AI. As we discussed, ethical concerns like bias and lack of transparency can cause discriminatory outcomes and break trust in AI systems. Similarly, failing to prioritize data privacy can turn away users and expose your business to legal risks.

As you move forward with AI in your business, remember that AI is the future of businesses and the world around us. Adopting ethical principles, prioritizing data privacy, and promoting a culture of responsible AI development can help you achieve sustainable success while leaving a positive impact on society.

Conclusion

Throughout this book, we have explored the wonders of AI—that is, how business decisions are backed by data insights, repetitive tasks are automated, and marketing campaigns generate leads with better precision. This is the reality within reach for businesses that leverage artificial intelligence (AI)'s potential at all levels of their operation.

However, AI is not a luxury reserved for tech giants; it is a toolkit accessible to businesses of all sizes. You no longer need to spend excess time over endless spreadsheets and struggle to gain information from mountains of data. AI-powered analytics tools can now crunch those numbers in seconds, revealing hidden patterns that inform smarter decision-making. Content creation, once a time-consuming effort, can be easy with AI that generates targeted marketing copy, product descriptions, or even personalized social media posts. The repetitive tasks that bog down your team's productivity—

data entry, scheduling meetings, or generating reports—can be automated with AI, allowing your employees to concentrate on what they do best: strategic thinking, creative problem-solving, and building meaningful customer relationships.

The impact of AI extends far beyond the back office. Your marketing campaigns can now target demographics, specific customer behaviors, and interests. Personalized product recommendations based on past purchases, customer service powered by AI chatbots that understand natural language, and pricing strategies that adjust based on market demand—these are just a few ways AI can transform the way you interact with your customers. A more personalized and effortless experience can help build customer loyalty and trust, leading to long-term business success.

However, with great power comes great responsibility. As we have discussed in the later chapter of this book, ethical consid-erations, and data privacy are paramount when implementing AI. Building trust with your customers and stakeholders requires a commitment to responsible AI practices. This means ensuring fairness and transparency in AI decisions, prioritizing data security, and remaining mindful of the potential impact of AI on society.

Remember Amazon? This e-commerce giant has leveraged AI not just for product recommendations but also for logistics and inventory management. It processes its data to predict customer demand and optimize inventory levels, ensuring products are readily available when customers need them. This translates into a smoother customer experience, reduces waste, and optimizes costs for Amazon.

The success story of Amazon is just one example of the benefits of AI for retail giants, businesses of all sizes, and across all industries. Whether you are a healthcare provider using AI to analyze patient data for faster diagnoses, a manufacturer using AI to predict equipment failure and prevent downtime, or a financial institution using AI to facilitate loan applications, the opportunities are endless.

Start the journey of integrating AI into every aspect of your business today. Let this book be your guide to implementing AI in a way that propels your business forward and does so with ethical integrity and respect for privacy—the true markers of lasting success. The future is bright for businesses that use AI responsibly, and I hope this book has equipped you with the knowledge and confidence to be a part of it.

AI has been a tremendous benefit to my business and me; however, there's one thing that AI cannot replace: genuine human interaction. With that being said, can I ask you a personal favor? You can make a real difference by sharing your review on Amazon. I am deeply touched by the kindness of my readers and would love to hear your experiences, too. Genuine reviews left by real people sharing real experiences help ensure trustworthiness to prospective readers. AI is a fantastic tool, but it can't replace human insight. But we can leverage it tremendously to build your business. Thank you for your support—it means a lot.

References

"541+ Top ChatGPT Prompts for Content Creation for Best Result," September 16, 2023. https://chatgptaihub.com/chatgpt-prompts-for-content-creation/.

"70 Useful ChatGPT Prompts for Marketing." Rodeo Software B.V., September 25, 2023. https://www.getrodeo.io/blog/chatgpt-prompts-for-marketing.

"The Rise of AI Content Creation: What It Means for Writers." AIContentfy, May 26, 2023. https://aicontentfy.com/en/blog/rise-of-ai-content-creation-what-it-means-for-writers.

"What Is Artificial Intelligence (AI)? | IBM," March 19, 2024. https://www.ibm.com/topics/artificial-intelligence.

AIContenfy Team. "The Benefits of AI in Content Creation: Enhancing Efficiency and Quality." AIContentfy, September 18, 2023. https://aicontentfy.com/en/blog/benefits-of-ai-in-content-creation-enhancing-efficiency-and-quality.

AIContenfyTeam. "ChatGPT and the Future of Customer Service." AIContentfy, January 27, 2023. https://aicontentfy.com/en/blog/chatgpt-and-future-of-customer-service.

AIContentfy Team. "The Future of Content Collaboration with AI-Powered Tools." AIContentfy, February 18, 2023. https://aicontentfy.com/en/blog/future-of-content-collaboration-with-ai-powered-tools.

Akshita. "100+ ChatGPT Prompts to Elevate Your Content Game," January 11, 2024. https://narrato.io/blog/100-chatgpt-prompts-for-content-creation-to-get-the-best-outputs/.

Alloba. "The Benefits of Using AI in Data Analysis," n.d. https://www.alooba.com/articles/benefits-of-using-ai-in-data-analysis/.

Alston, Elena. "How to Automate ChatGPT," April 8, 2024. https://zapier.com/blog/automate-chatgpt/.

Arshad, Umar. "49+ Best ChatGPT Prompts for Leads Generation in 2024 (Boost Conversion)," October 8, 2023. https://chatgptaihub.com/chatgpt-prompts-for-leads-generation/.

avcontentteam. "Top 20 AI and Machine Learning Trends to Watch in

2024." *Analytics Vidhya* (blog), May 1, 2023. https://www.analyticsvidhya. com/blog/2023/05/emerging-trends-in-ai-and-machine-learning/.

Babich, Nick. "How to Use ChatGPT in Product Design: 8 Practical Examples." Medium, January 4, 2023. https://uxplanet.org/how-to-use-chatgpt-in-product-design-8-practical-examples-a6135308b9b2.

Baker, Kristen. "10 Proven Ways to Use ChatGPT for Business for Growth." Podium, October 19, 2023. https://www.podium.com/article/ways-to-use-chatgpt-for-business/.

Bashir, Iman. "8 Reasons Using AI Will Improve Your Content Creation Process." Entrepreneur, June 15, 2022. https://www.entrepreneur.com/lead ership/8-reasons-using-ai-will-improve-your-content-creation/426695.

Bhanu Teja, P. "How To Set Up A Customer Service Chatbot ChatGPT." SiteGPT, October 28, 2023. https://sitegpt.ai/blog/customer-service-chatbot-chatgpt.

Blackman, Reid. "A Practical Guide to Building Ethical AI." *Harvard Business Review*, October 15, 2020. https://hbr.org/2020/10/a-practical-guide-to-building-ethical-ai.

Bossmann, Julia. "Top 9 Ethical Issues in Artificial Intelligence." World Economic Forum, October 21, 2016. https://www.weforum.org/agenda/ 2016/10/top-10-ethical-issues-in-artificial-intelligence/.

Bowman, Jeremy. "10 Top Companies Using AI." The Motley Fool, n.d. https:// www.fool.com/investing/stock-market/market-sectors/information-tech nology/ai-stocks/companies-that-use-ai/.

Brandon, Samantha. "5 Ways to Power Up Your Content Marketing With AI." StoryChief - Content Marketing Blog, n.d. https://storychief.io/blog/ power-up-content-marketing-with-ai.

Bungsy, Agnes. "ChatGPT Prompts for Data Analysis." AnalyticsHacker, n.d. https://www.analyticshacker.com/analytics-resources/ai-prompts-for-data-analysis.

Calzon, Bernardita. "The Importance of Data Driven Decision Making for Business," November 17, 2022. https://www.datapine.com/blog/data-driven-decision-making-in-businesses/.

ClickUp. "ChatGPT Prompts For Data Analysis," n.d. https://clickup.com/ templates/ai-prompts/data-analysis.

ClickUp. "ChatGPT Prompts For Lead Generation," n.d. https://clickup.com/ templates/ai-prompts/lead-generation.

ClickUp. "ChatGPT Prompts For Project Scheduling," n.d. https://clickup.com/ templates/ai-prompts/project-scheduling.

ClickUp. "ChatGPT Prompts For Team Meetings," n.d. https://clickup.com/templates/ai-prompts/team-meetings.

Copeland, B.J. "Artificial Intelligence (AI) | Definition, Examples, Types, Applications, Companies, & Facts | Britannica," April 29, 2024. https://www.britannica.com/technology/artificial-intelligence.

Council of Europe: Artificial Intelligence. "History of Artificial Intelligence - Artificial Intelligence," n.d. https://www.coe.int/en/web/artificial-intelligence/history-of-ai.

Council of Europe: Human Rights and Biomedicine. "Common Ethical Challenges in AI," n.d. https://www.coe.int/en/web/bioethics/common-ethical-challenges-in-ai.

Crabtree, Matt. "How to Use ChatGPT for Sales." Datacamp, June 2023. https://www.datacamp.com/tutorial/how-to-use-chat-gpt-for-sales.

Craig, Lindsay. "How to Use ChatGPT to Generate Product Ideas & Marketing Campaigns." *Medium* (blog), December 15, 2022. https://lindsay-craig.medium.com/how-to-use-chatgpt-3-to-generate-product-ideas-marketing-campaigns-204dee40ab1d.

Dasha. "Why Understanding Customer Needs Through AI Is Crucial," December 7, 2023. https://dasha.ai/en-us/blog/why-understanding-customer-needs-through-ai-is-crucial.

dealcode. "ChatGPT for Sales: 7 Ways to Boost Your Sales Process | Dealcode," May 11, 2023. https://www.dealcode.ai/blog/chatgpt-for-sales-7-ways-to-boost-your-sales-process.

Derungs, Amy. "ChatGPT for Copywriting: 10 Easy Ways To Boost Conversions in 2024." Niche Pursuits, April 27, 2023. https://www.nichepursuits.com/chatgpt-for-copywriting/.

Describely. "Free Resource: 30+ Time Saving Ecommerce ChatGPT Prompts." Describely, October 11, 2023. https://describely.ai/blog/chatgpt-ecommerce-prompts/.

Document360 Team. "8 Use Cases of ChatGPT for Customer Service." Document360, May 19, 2023. https://document360.com/blog/chatgpt-for-customer-service/.

Dr Mark van Rijmenam, CSP | Strategic Futurist Speaker. "Privacy in the Age of AI: Risks, Challenges and Solutions," February 16, 2023. https://www.thedigitalspeaker.com/privacy-age-ai-risks-challenges-solutions/.

Dragonfly AI. "How to Use AI in Graphic Design," n.d. https://dragonflyai.co/resources/blog/how-to-use-ai-to-inform-design.

Dutta, DataStax, Deb. "Unlocking the Power of Data Analysis with ChatGPT." CDO Trends, September 18, 2023. https://www.cdotrends.com/story/18409/unlocking-power-data-analysis-chatgpt.

Ecommerce Prompts. "ChatGPT Prompts for the Ultimate Ecommerce Marketer," n.d. https://www.ecommerceprompts.com/.

Editorial Team. "How to Use ChatGPT to Write Marketing Copy," March 20, 2024. https://dorik.com/blog/how-to-use-chatgpt-to-write-marketing-copy.

Fitzpatrick, Klarissa. "AI in Sales and Marketing: What Is It?" Ringover, June 26, 2023. https://www.ringover.com/blog/ai-in-sales-marketing.

Five Star Visibility. "How to Use an AI Chatbot to Increase Customer Satisfaction for Your Small Business." LinkedIn, January 5, 2024. https://www.linkedin.com/pulse/how-use-ai-chatbot-increase-customer-satisfaction-your-ldkke.

Flores, Brian. "5 Ways Generative AI Fosters and Improves Team Collaboration." Agility PR Solutions, October 18, 2023. https://www.agilitypr.com/pr-news/public-relations/5-ways-generative-ai-fosters-and-improves-team-collaboration/.

Gandía, Rafa. "10 Ways to Generate Leads with ChatGPT in Seconds." *FindThatLead* (blog), January 31, 2023. https://blog.findthatlead.com/en/generate-leads-with-chatgpt.

Georgiou, Michael. "30+ Key Business Automation Statistics You Should Know." Imaginovation | Top Web & Mobile App Development Company Raleigh, n.d. https://imaginovation.net/blog/business-automation-statistics/.

Gerrard + Bizway AI Assistant. "11 Helpful ChatGPT Prompts for Report Writing (December 2023)," December 18, 2023. https://www.bizway.io/blog/chatgpt-prompts-for-report-writing.

Greenan, Richard. "ChatGPT for UX Design: The Top 15 Prompts," July 25, 2023. https://careerfoundry.com/en/blog/ux-design/chatgpt-for-ux-design/.

Guest Author. "8 Surprising Benefits of AI in Team Collaboration You Might Not Realize." Stormboard, August 4, 2023. https://stormboard.com/blog/8-surprising-benefits-of-ai-in-team-collaboration.

Guinness, Harry. "How to Use ChatGPT for Copywriting and Content Ideation," May 31, 2023. https://zapier.com/blog/chatgpt-marketing-writing/.

Gunn, Elliot. "11 of the Best ChatGPT Data Analysis Prompts You Should Know," July 28, 2023. https://careerfoundry.com/en/blog/data-analytics/data-analysis-prompts/.

Gupta, Pragati. "ChatGPT Prompts for E-Commerce That You Can Check out in 2023." The Writesonic Blog - Making Content Your Superpower, April 29, 2023. https://writesonic.com/blog/chatgpt-prompts-ecommerce/.

Hari, Jishnu. "10 Powerful Ways to Use ChatGPT as a Product Designer." Medium, April 18, 2023. https://uxdesign.cc/10-powerful-ways-to-use-chatgpt-as-a-product-designer-b3c395d20a00.

Hariri, Farah. "20 Ingenuis ChatGPT Prompts for UX & Product Designers." Medium, February 3, 2023. https://bootcamp.uxdesign.cc/20-ingenuis-chatgpt-prompts-for-ux-product-designers-1ffca0b451fa.

Harry's Blockchain Blog. "Unlocking the Potential of ChatGPT for Inventory Management: Our Roadmap with ChatGPT." *Medium* (blog), February 3, 2023. https://medium.com/gearchain/unlocking-the-potential-of-chatgpt-for-inventory-management-our-roadmap-with-chatgpt-9a5071cb1bbe.

Helpwise. "50 Expert-Approved ChatGPT Prompts For Customer Service Challenges," May 22, 2023. https://helpwise.io/blog/chatgpt-prompts-for-customer-service.

Helpwise. "The Complete Guide to Using ChatGPT for Customer Service," May 5, 2023. https://helpwise.io/blog/how-to-use-chatgpt-for-customer-service.

Hines, Kristi. "History Of ChatGPT: A Timeline Of The Meteoric Rise Of Generative AI Chatbots." Search Engine Journal, June 4, 2023. https://www.searchenginejournal.com/history-of-chatgpt-timeline/488370/.

Hirsch, Dennis, and Piers Norris Turner. "What Is 'Ethical AI' and How Can Companies Achieve It?" The Conversation, May 25, 2023. http://theconversation.com/what-is-ethical-ai-and-how-can-companies-achieve-it-204349.

Howarth, John. "57 NEW AI Statistics (Apr 2024)." Exploding Topics, August 17, 2021. https://explodingtopics.com/blog/ai-statistics.

Inclusion Digital Engineering. "10 Steps to More Ethical Artificial Intelligence," March 17, 2023. https://inclusioncloud.com/insights/blog/ethical-artificial-intelligence/.

Innovation at Work. "Three Ways To Prepare Your Workforce for Artificial Intelligence." *IEEE Innovation at Work* (blog), September 8, 2021. https://innovationatwork.ieee.org/three-ways-to-prepare-your-workforce-for-artificial-intelligence/.

Ipsen, Adam. "ChatGPT's Code Interpreter Is Now Advanced Data Analysis," September 20, 2023. https://www.pluralsight.com/resources/blog/data/ChatGPT-Advanced-Data-Analytics.

James. "10 ChatGPT Email Prompts to Boost Your Email Performance." Mailbutler, May 19, 2023. https://www.mailbutler.io/blog/email/chatgpt-email-prompts/.

Jasaitis, Algirdas. "Top 10 Best Business Report Chatgpt Prompt Example 2024." WPS Blog, August 3, 2023. https://www.wps.com/blog/top-10-best-business-report-chatgpt-prompt-example-2023-1/.

Jenni. "Chat GPT in Data Analysis: Unlocking the Future of Research," October 30, 2023. https://jenni.ai/chat-gpt/research-data-analysis-uses.

Joy, F. "40 ChatGPT AI Prompts for Stellar Lead Generation," September 7, 2023. https://themarketinghustle.com/ai-marketing/40-chatgpt-ai-prompts-for-stellar-lead-generation/.

Kanev, Kal. "Responsible AI: How to Make Your Enterprise Ethical, so That Your AI Is Too." DXC Technology, n.d. https://dxc.com/us/en/insights/perspectives/paper/responsible-ai.

Karp, Ethan. "ChatGPT Swears It Can Optimize Your Inventory. Let's Examine." Forbes, March 1, 2023. https://www.forbes.com/sites/ethankarp/2023/03/01/chatgpt-swears-it-can-optimize-your-inventory-lets-examine/.

Kempton, Beth. "How Is AI Used in Business? 10 Ways It Can Help." Upwork, August 11, 2023. https://www.upwork.com/resources/how-is-ai-used-in-business.

Kleinings, Hanna. "How to Get the Most out of AI in 2023: 7 Applications of Artificial Intelligence in Business." Levity, January 18, 2023. https://levity.ai/blog/8-uses-ai-business.

Lazarevikj, Oliver. "10 Powerful Ways to Use ChatGPT as a Product Designer." Visual Side (blog), March 20, 2023. https://medium.com/visual-side/10-powerful-ways-to-use-chatgpt-as-a-product-designer-caee567d9dcb.

Leadership AI. "20 Ultimate ChatGPT Prompts for Team Leaders." Spinach.io, October 25, 2023. https://www.spinach.io/blog/best-chatgpt-prompts-for-team-leaders.

Lee, Alvin. "How to Protect Data Privacy When Using AI." Twilio, November 13, 2023. https://www.twilio.com/en-us/blog/ai-data-privacy.

LIGS University. "The Role of Artificial Intelligence in Improving Project

Management," August 6, 2020. https://ligsuniversity.com/blog/the-role-of-artificial-intelligence-in-improving-project-management.

Lile, Samantha. "50 Best ChatGPT Prompts for Communications Workflows." Simpplr, January 29, 2024. https://www.simpplr.com/blog/2024/chatgpt-communication-prompts/.

LinkedIn. "Essential Chat GPT Prompts for Designers," August 23, 2023. https://www.linkedin.com/pulse/essential-chat-gpt-prompts-designers-designwithpro.

LinkedIn. "How Can Artificial Intelligence Enhance Conceptual Design Feedback?," December 6, 2023. https://www.linkedin.com/advice/0/how-can-artificial-intelligence-enhance-conceptual-design-h6a6e.

LinkedIn. "How Can You Stay Up-to-Date with the Latest Research in Artificial Intelligence?" n.d. https://www.linkedin.com/advice/3/how-can-you-stay-up-to-date-latest-research-1c.

LinkedIn. "How Do You Keep up with the Latest Trends and Innovations in AI?" January 17, 2024. https://www.linkedin.com/advice/3/how-do-you-keep-up-latest-trends-innovations-7041842070671556608.

Lundberg, Steph. "Benefits of AI in Customer Service: 4 Ways AI Can Help." Help Scout, n.d. https://www.helpscout.com/blog/benefits-of-ai-in-customer-service/.

Macready, Hannah. "65 ChatGPT Prompts for Marketing to Make Work Easier." Social Media Marketing & Management Dashboard, July 25, 2023. https://blog.hootsuite.com/chatgpt-prompts-for-marketing/.

Maderis, Giana. "Top 22 Benefits of Chatbots for Businesses and Customers." Zendesk, November 20, 2019. https://www.zendesk.com/blog/5-benefits-using-ai-bots-customer-service/.

Mailbutler. "ChatGPT Email Prompts," November 1, 2023. https://www.linkedin.com/pulse/chatgpt-email-prompts-mailbutler-gmbh-uhjze.

Majumder, Deepa. "Top Benefits of AI-Powered Service Desk." workativ.com, n.d. https://workativ.comfalse.

Mandula, Mark S. "What Kind of Training Could I Do for My Employees on AI/GenAI?" LinkedIn, September 14, 2023. https://www.linkedin.com/pulse/what-kind-training-could-i-do-my-employees-aigenai-mark-s-mandula.

Marr, Bernard. "The 10 Best Examples Of How Companies Use Artificial Intelligence In Practice." *Bernard Marr* (blog), July 2, 2021. https://bernardmarr.com/the-10-best-examples-of-how-companies-use-artificial-intelli

gence-in-practice/.

Martin, Michelle. "10 AI Content Creation Tools That Will Make Your Job Easier." Social Media Marketing & Management Dashboard, October 5, 2023. https://blog.hootsuite.com/ai-powered-content-creation/.

Maryville University. "AI in Business: Ethical Considerations," March 28, 2023. https://online.maryville.edu/blog/ai-ethical-issues/.

Mason, Scott. "4 Ways to Use AI in Content Marketing (Plus Examples)." GLC | Your Audience Awaits, September 16, 2022. https://glcdelivers.com/4-ways-to-use-ai-in-content-marketing-plus-examples/.

McKay, Sam. "ChatGPT Advanced Data Analysis: Explained | Master Data Skills + AI," September 26, 2023. https://blog.enterprisedna.co/chatgpt-advanced-data-analysis-explained/.

Medairy, Brad. "4 Ways to Preserve Privacy in Artificial Intelligence," n.d. https://www.boozallen.com/s/solution/four-ways-to-preserve-privacy-in-ai.html.

Melara, Ale. "Exploring the Benefits and Limitations of Using AI for Content Creation." SmartBug., April 25, 2023. https://www.smartbugmedia.com/blog/benefits-and-limitations-of-ai-for-content-creation.

Mike Paul. "How to Stay Up-to-Date on the Latest AI Trends," May 14, 2023. https://techpilot.ai/how-to-stay-up-to-date-on-the-latest-ai-trends/.

MIT Management. "How to Use ChatGPT's Advanced Data Analysis Feature." *MIT Sloan Teaching & Learning Technologies* (blog), n.d. https://mitsloanedtech.mit.edu/ai/tools/data-analysis/how-to-use-chatgpts-advanced-data-analysis-feature/.

MonkeyLearn. "What Is Data Analysis and How Can You Get Started?" MonkeyLearn, n.d. https://monkeylearn.com/data-analysis/.

Moulton, Luke. "7 Ways ChatGPT Can Help with Lead Generation | LeadSync," March 24, 2023. https://leadsync.me/blog/chatgpt-lead-generation/.

Nawab, Alsabah. "How Can We Use ChatGPT to Automate Workflows?" n.d. https://www.linkedin.com/pulse/how-can-we-use-chatgpt-automate-workflows-alsabah-nawab.

Neher, Krista. "Council Post: Five Ways To Get Your Employees AI Ready." Forbes, January 9, 2024. https://www.forbes.com/sites/forbescoachescouncil/2024/01/09/five-ways-to-get-your-employees-ai-ready/.

Newberry, Christina. "74 Artificial Intelligence Statistics to Guide Your Marketing Plan." Social Media Marketing & Management Dashboard, August 16, 2023. https://blog.hootsuite.com/artificial-intelligence-statistics/.

Nyman, Cheryl. "Launching Your AI Journey: Four Essential Steps to Success." BPM, November 7, 2023. https://www.bpm.com/insights/how-to-start-your-ai-journey/.

Oana. "10 Key Benefits of Business Process Automation." Penneo, February 10, 2021. https://penneo.com/blog/10-benefits-business-process-automation/.

Overvest, Marijn. "ChatGPT Inventory — Using AI to Optimize Stock Levels." *Procurement Tactics* (blog), November 27, 2023. https://procurement tactics.com/chatgpt-inventory/.

OVIC: Office of the Victorian Information Commissioner. "Artificial Intelligence and Privacy – Issues and Challenges," n.d. https://ovic.vic.gov. au/privacy/resources-for-organisations/artificial-intelligence-and-privacy-issues-and-challenges/.

Padmavati. "Building Stronger Teams With ChatGPT." Northwest Executive Education, June 13, 2023. https://northwest.education/insights/careers/building-stronger-teams-with-chatgpt/.

Pappas, Christopher. "The Role Of AI In The Future Of Project Management." eLearning Industry, October 2, 2023. https://elearningindustry.com/role-of-ai-in-the-future-of-project-management.

Petit, Maria. "AI Project Management: The Future of Efficient Project Execution." Monitask, November 21, 2023. https://www.monitask.com/en/blog/the-role-of-artificial-intelligence-in-improving-project-management-how-ai-can-help-make-projects-run-smoothly.

Podium Staff. "AI Chatbot for Customer Service: How To Do It Right With 10 Examples." Podium, n.d. https://www.podium.com/article/ai-chatbot-for-customer-service-how-to-do-it-right/.

Porter, Jon. "ChatGPT Continues to Be One of the Fastest-Growing Services Ever." The Verge, November 6, 2023. https://www.theverge.com/2023/11/6/23948386/chatgpt-active-user-count-openai-developer-conference.

PricewaterhouseCoopers. "6 Generative AI Business Myths That Will Make You Rethink Everything." PwC, n.d. https://www.pwc.com/us/en/tech-effect/ai-analytics/six-generative-ai-business-myths.html.

Pro AI Prompt. ". Generating Team Collaboration Workflows ChatGPT Prompts - Pro AI Prompt," December 12, 2023. https://proaiprompt.com/generating-team-collaboration-workflows-chatgpt-prompts/.

process.st. "How to Automate Business Processes In 6 Simple Steps (+ Tools List)," July 13, 2023. https://www.process.st/how-to-automate-business-processes/.

Proprompter Editor. "ChatGPT Prompts for Report Writing ." *ProPromter* (blog), October 3, 2023. https://proprompter.com/chatgpt-prompts-for-report-writing/.

Randolph, Kevin. "AI for Sales: Benefits, Challenges, and How You Can Use It." Nutshell, May 11, 2023. https://www.nutshell.com/blog/ai-for-sales.

Repaka, Ram Sekhar. "How to Integrate ChatGPT with Ecommerce Website?" Ram Sekhar Repaka, March 4, 2023. https://www.ramsekharrepaka.com/post/how-to-integrate-chatgpt-with-ecommerce-website.

Repin, Stefan. "AI-Powered Forecasting: Use AI to Predict Future Market Trends, Sales Performance, and Customer Behavior." Platforce, November 23, 2023. https://platforce.io/ai-powered-forecasting-use-ai-to-predict-future-market-trends-sales-performance-and-customer-behavior/.

Roberti, Damian. "Implementing ChatGPT for Effective Inventory Management." Marketing Food Online, April 20, 2023. https://marketing foodonline.com/blogs/news/implementing-chatgpt-for-effective-inventory-management.

Robinson, Ryan. "Content Marketing AI: How to Make the Most of It | Zapier," October 5, 2023. https://zapier.com/blog/content-marketing-ai/.

Rockwell, Anyoha. "The History of Artificial Intelligence." *Science in the News* (blog), August 28, 2017. https://sitn.hms.harvard.edu/flash/2017/history-artificial-intelligence/.

Samuel. "AI-Assisted Collaboration: Empower Your Team with ChatGPT!" *Collection Performance* (blog), April 17, 2023. https://collection performance.com/collaboration-with-chatgpt/.

SendBoard. "50 Useful ChatGPT Prompts To Boost Your Email Writing Productivity," n.d. https://www.sendboard.com/blog/chat-gpt-prompts.

Seth, Huang. "How ChatGPT Helps Teams Be Better Communicators - and Everyone Is Happier for It," March 8, 2023. https://www.linkedin.com/pulse/how-chatgpt-helps-teams-better-communicators-seth-huang-ph-d-.

Shivani, D. "How Do You Identify and Prioritize the Most Suitable Business Processes for Automation?" LinkedIn, n.d. https://www.linkedin.com/advice/0/how-do-you-identify-prioritize-most-suitable.

Sidor, Jonathan. "50+ Top Stats on AI in Customer Service for 2024," December 28, 2023. https://getzowie.com/blog/stats-ai-customer-service.

Simplilearn. "What Is Data Analysis: A Comprehensive Guide." Simplilearn.com, May 27, 2020. https://www.simplilearn.com/data-analy

sis-methods-process-types-article.

Singh, Dilip. "How to Use Chatgpt for Product Development." LinkedIn, April 16, 2023. https://www.linkedin.com/pulse/how-use-chatgpt-product-devel opment-dilip-singh.

Smarty, Ann. "ChatGPT Prompts for Customer Support." *Practical Ecommerce* (blog), May 30, 2023. https://www.practicalecommerce.com/ chatgpt-prompts-for-customer-support.

Smulders, Stefan. "Chat GPT For B2B Sales & Lead Generation: The Ultimate Guide." *Expandi* (blog), August 8, 2023. https://expandi.io/blog/use-chat gpt-for-lead-generation/.

Snook, Jason. "How Businesses Can Start Their AI Journey." CapTech, May 12, 2023. https://www.captechconsulting.com/articles/how-businesses-can start-on-their-ai-journey.

Spisak, Brian, Louis B. Rosenberg, and Max Beilby. "13 Principles for Using AI Responsibly." *Harvard Business Review*, June 30, 2023. https://hbr.org/2023/ 06/13-principles-for-using-ai-responsibly.

Stobierski, Tim. "The Advantages of Data-Driven Decision-Making." Business Insights Blog, August 26, 2019. https://online.hbs.edu/blog/post/data driven-decision-making.

Tamilore, June. "6 Applications of AI for Content Creation." Buffer: All-you-need social media toolkit for small businesses, June 4, 2023. https://buffer. com/resources/ai-content-creation/.

Team Kissflow. "20+ Key Business Process Automation Stats You Need To Know," April 8, 2024. https://kissflow.com/workflow/bpm/business process-automation-statistics/.

Team, OTS Marketing. "Business for AI | Top 10 Steps to Prepare Your Business for AI." OTS Solutions, February 14, 2019. https://otssolutions.com/top-10-steps-to-prepare-your-business-for-ai/.

The Investopedia Team. "What Is Artificial Intelligence (AI)?" Investopedia, April 9, 2024. https://www.investopedia.com/terms/a/artificial-intelli gence-ai.asp.

The Upwork Team. "The Top 8 Benefits of Business Process Automation." Upwork, April 12, 2023. https://www.upwork.com/resources/business process-automation-benefits.

todook. "AI Chatbot Implementation: Overcoming Challenges & Lessons," July 17, 2023. https://todook.io/overcoming-challenges-in-ai-chatbot-imple mentation-lessons-learned/.

Tsuei, Judy. "Optimize Your Calendar with ChatGPT." clockwise, May 31, 202AD. https://www.getclockwise.com/blog/chatgpt-calendar-optimization.

Tully, Maggie. "50 Practical ChatGPT Prompts for Project Management." Rodeo Software B.V., May 30, 2023. https://www.getrodeo.io/blog/chatgpt-prompts-for-project-management.

Tushar, Jain. "10 Best Chatgpt Prompts For Customer Service-2024." *Enthu.Ai* (blog), June 26, 2023. https://enthu.ai/blog/chatgpt-prompts-for-customer-service/.

Unbounce. "Break Free: The State of AI Marketing for Small Business," September 23, 2023. https://unbounce.com/ai-for-small-business-report/.

Unity Group. "Uncover 9 Myths About AI in Business," April 18, 2023. https://www.unitygroup.com/blog/ai-in-business-most-common-myths-debunked/.

Valchanov, Iliya. "Best 25 ChatGPT Prompts for Marketing in 2024." *Team-GPT* (blog), September 15, 2023. https://team-gpt.com/blog/chatgpt-prompts-for-marketing/.

Venkateswaran, Hari Narayanan. "How to Utilize Chatbots to Improve Customer Satisfaction." Customer Service Blog from HappyFox – Improve Customer Service & Experience, October 22, 2020. https://blog.happyfox.com/how-to-utilize-chatbots-to-improve-customer-satisfaction/.

Vishal, Dave. "ChatGPT For Content Writing: 20+ Prompts To Try," February 6, 2023. https://meetanshi.com/blog/chatgpt-for-content/.

Watters, Ashley. "11 Common Ethical Issues in Artificial Intelligence." CompTIA Community, November 16, 2023. https://connect.comptia.org/blog/common-ethical-issues-in-artificial-intelligence.

Way, Paul. "Top 5 Trends to Look Forward to in 2024 for Generative AI." Hitachi Solutions, December 19, 2023. https://global.hitachi-solutions.com/blog/5-generative-ai-trends-2024/.

Webster, Mark. "149 AI Statistics: The Present and Future of AI [2024 Stats]," May 24, 2023. https://www.authorityhacker.com/ai-statistics/.

Wharton Online. "How Do Businesses Use Artificial Intelligence?," January 19, 2022. https://online.wharton.upenn.edu/blog/how-do-businesses-use-artificial-intelligence/.

Wren, Hannah. "ChatGPT for Customer Service: A Complete Guide." Zendesk, October 17, 2023. https://www.zendesk.com/blog/chatgpt-for-customer-service/.

Wright, Verrion. "8 Generative AI Best Practices for Privacy." *BigID* (blog), October 26, 2023. https://bigid.com/blog/8-generative-ai-best-practices-for-privacy/.

Xeven, S. E. O. "How to Integrate ChatGPT with an E-Commerce Website." Xeven Solutions, August 8, 2023. https://www.xevensolutions.com/blog/the-uses-of-chatgpt-integration-with-an-e-commerce-website/.Webster,

M. (2024, January 10). 149 AI Statistics: The Present and Future of AI [2024 stats]. Authority Hacker. https://www.authorityhacker.com/ai-statistics/

www.ingramcontent.com/pod-product-compliance
Lightning Source LLC
Chambersburg PA
CBHW071604210326
41597CB00019B/3401